D1178096

A Cantonese Book

Third Edition

Chan Kwok Kin   **Betty Hung**

Greenwood Press

GREENWOOD PRESS

47 Pokfulam Road, 8/F, Hong Kong.

Tel: (852)2546 8212, (852)2547 7041

Email: gwpress@ctimail.com

Website: www.green-woodpress.com

First Edition 1995

Second Edition 2005

Third Edition November, 2009.

ISBN: 978-962-279-266-1

PRINTED IN HONG KONG

Preface

The first edition of '*A Cantonese Book*' was published in 1995. In 2005, a second edition was published to reflect the changes in lifestyle of the people in Hong Kong. This, the third edition, adds more dialogue and diversified exercises. However, as in the two previous editions, the style remains simple, practical and interesting. We, the authors, hope that this edition will continue to be well-received by teachers and students around the world.

We hope that all our students enjoy learning Cantonese. Finallly, may we wish you every success as you build up confidence in speaking the language.

We welcome suggestions and comments.

The authors

Contents

How to use this book

This book is divided into 16 lessons. It is based on actual situations in Hong Kong. The text used is suitable for communication with other Cantonese speakers, be they in Guangzhou, Singapore or in any Chinatown in any corner of the world.

The book is written in Chinese characters with Romanization (Yale system) also provided. The Chinese characters will help students to communicate with other Cantonese speakers, and they will also help those who can already read Chinese to progress faster. Yale Romanization is the most popular system for teaching foreigners. Dictionaries and textbooks using this system are readily found.

This book covers some 45 grammatical points and over 300 items of vocabulary; all of which are presented in a step-by-step format. Related vocabulary and cultural notes are provided to stimulate interest and increase awareness of the environment in Hong Kong.

Lessons 1-4: cover useful daily expressions; such as numbers, greetings, time expressions and directions for travelling by taxi. These simple phrases encourage the use of Cantonese in daily life. Students are encouraged to try them out whenever and wherever possible. Those courageous enough will be gently surprised at how their listeners respond with beaming smiles of delight.

Lessons 5-7 are short conversations: to introduce yourself to your friends and acquaintances. They also give you the basic vocabulary for shopping and buying food and drink. Basic Cantonese structures are gradually introduced.

Lessons 8-16: students begin to build up their knowledge of Cantonese grammar. These lessons focus on developing the student's ability to speak in full sentences and progress towards describing happenings and situations. Each lesson is divided into the following sections:

Conversation: Topics are carefully chosen, based on real life situations. They serve as a summary of the sentence patterns which have already been introduced. An English translation is provided.

Reading: Short passages are given as a variation to conversation. Students learn to describe an incident or express ideas.

Vocabulary: New words or phrases are introduced. In the right hand column, the parts of speech and English equivalents are given. Examples of common usage are also given. The new vocabulary is reinforced in later lessons.

Abbreviations of parts of speech:

ADJ	adjective
ADV	adverb
AV	auxilary verb
CON	conjunction
FP	final particle
IE	idomatic expressions
M	measure
N	noun
NU	number
P	particle
PH	phrase
PN	pronoun
PW	place word
QW	question word
SP	specifier
TW	time word

V   verb

VO   verb object compound

VS   verb suffix

Sentence Patterns: All new grammatical structures are highlighted in boxes and they are followed by various forms of the patterns. Copious examples and practice pieces are also given.. The English equivalent of any new word is given inside brackets and highlighted with an asterisk*.

e.g. dím-gáai (*why)

Pyramid drills and substitution drills: This refers to a review of key vocabulary and sentence patterns.

Review exercises: Written and oral exercises given. The oral exercises include answering questions, creating conversations and participating in games. The written exercises include filling in blanks, rewriting sentences, and translation.

Listening exercises: The student listens to conversations and then answers questions. Most questions are multiple choice. There are about 12 questions in each lesson.

Appendices are attached at the end of the book.

Appendix 1 & 2 contain a list of vocabulary, in alphabetical order. Two forms are supplied : Cantonese to English, and English to Cantonese. The lesson in which each piece of vocabulary appears is also indicated.

Appendix 3 consists of Cantonese slang and local sayings. This appendix is intended to give students a better understanding of Hong Kong society and culture.

Romanization system

Each syllabus of Cantonese is composed of three elements:

1. Initial: the beginning sound element of a syllable. There are 19 initials in all.

2. Finial: the ending sound element of a syllable or a vowel. There are 51 finals in all.

3. Tone: the relative pitch, or variation of pitch, of a syllable. There are 7 tones in all.

An example of a syllable:

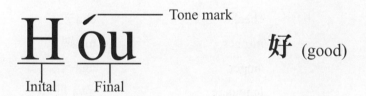

好 (good)

An example of a syllable:

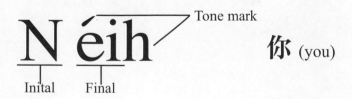

你 (you)

INITIALS   *(Track 001)*

		as in English	*example*
1.	B	boy	ba 巴
2.	P	park	pa 扒
3.	D	dig	da 打
4.	T	till	ta 他
5.	G	game	ga 加
6.	K	kill	ka 卡
7.	F	far	fa 花
8.	H	home	ha 哈
9.	N	no	na 那
10.	L	law	la 啦
11.	J	jam	ja 揸
12.	Ch	check	cha 差
13.	M	mother	ma 媽
14.	Ng	singer	nga 牙
15.	Gw	language	gwa 瓜
16.	Kw	quite	kwa 誇
17.	S	sand	sa 沙
18.	W	water	wa 娃
19.	Y	yes	ya 也

FINALS

		as in English	*example*	*(meaning)*
AA	*(Track 002)*			
1.	a	father	chā 叉	(fork)
2.	aai	aisle	daaih 大	(big)
3.	aau	owl	gaau 教	(teach)
4.	aam	arm	sāam 衫	(clothes)
5.	aan	aunt	fàan 返	(return)
6.	aang	Hong Kong (American pronunciation)	sàang 生	(raw)
7.	aap	harp ("p" mute) (tongue not curled)	jaahp 閘	(gate)
8.	aat	art ("t" mute) (tongue not curled)	baat 八	(eight)
9.	aak	ark ("k" mute) (tongue not curled)	baak 百	(hundred)

A	*(Track 003)*			
10.	ai	sight	sai 細	(small)
11.	au	out ("t" mute)	gau 夠	(enough)
12.	am	sum	sām 心	(heart)
13.	an	sun	fàn 分	(minute)
14.	ang	dung	dáng 等	(wait)
15.	ap	up ("p" mute)	jāp 汁	(juice)
16.	at	but ("t" mute)	bāt 筆	(pen)
17.	ak	duck ("k" mute)	bāk 北	(north)

E *(Track 004)*

18.	e	yes	jē 遮	(umbrella)
19.	eng	leng	geng 鏡	(mirror)
20.	ek	echo	tek 踢	(kick)
21.	ei	day	béi 畀	(give)

EU *(Track 005)*

22.	eu	her (tongue not curled)	hèu 靴	(boot)
23.	eung	ear (ni)ng	lèuhng 涼	(cool)
24.	euk	turk ("k" mute) (tongue not curled)	geuk 腳	(foot)
25.	eui	deuil (in French)	heui 去	(go)
26.	eun	(nat) ion	seun 信	(letter)
27.	eut	no equivalent	chēut 出	(out)

I *(Track 006)*

28.	i	bee	si 試	(try)
29.	iu	"ee" + "oo"	siu 笑	(smile)
30.	im	seem	dím 點	(o'clock)
31.	in	seen	sìn 先	(first)
32.	ip	jeep ("p" mute)	díp 碟	(dish)
33.	it	seat ("t" mute)	yiht 熱	(hot)
34.	ing	sing	bìng 冰	(ice)
35.	ik	sick ("k" mute)	sīk 識	(know)

O   *(Track 007)*

36.	o	orchard	cho 錯	(wrong)
37.	oi	boy	choi 菜	(vegetables)
38.	on	on	gòn 乾	(dry)
39.	ong	song	tòng 湯	(soup)
40.	ot	ought ("t" mute)	hot 渴	(thirsty)
41.	ok	awkward ("k" mute)	gwok 國	(country)
42.	ou	toe	hóu 好	(good)

U   *(Track 008)*

43.	u	fruit	fú 苦	(bitter)
44.	ui	"oo" + "ee"	būi 杯	(cup)
45.	un	soon	wún 碗	(bowl)
46.	ut	boot ("t" mute)	fut 闊	(wide)
47.	ung	tongue (N. English)	jūng 鐘	(clock)
48.	uk	hook ("k" mute)	ūk 屋	(house)

YU   *(Track 009)*

49.	yu	Dessus (in French)	syù 書	(book)
50.	yun	Une (in French)	syùn 酸	(sour)
51.	yut	chute (in French)	syut 雪	(snow)

TONES   *(Track 010)*

The following is a sketch illustrating the co-relation of the seven tones in Cantonese:

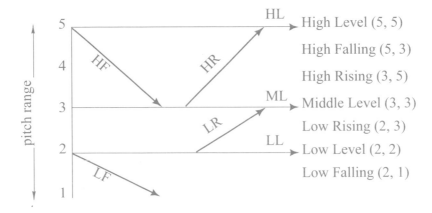

It is important to note that a sound in a certain tone may differ in meaning from the same sound in another tone. (The following is an example.)

Name of Tone	Tone mark	Example
High Level	with '-' on top of first vowel	sī 詩 (poem)
High Falling	with '`' on top of first vowel	sì 撕 (to tear)
High Rising	with '´' on top of first vowel	sí 史 (history)
Middle Level	none	si 試 (to try)
Low Falling	with '`' on top, an 'h' after the vowel(s)	sìh 時 (time)
Low Rising	with '´' on top, an 'h' after the vowel(s)	síh 市 (market)
Low Level	with an 'h' after the vowel(s)	sih 事 (matter)

SIMILAR INITIAL DRILL

'b' and 'p'   *(Track 011)*

1. báau 飽   páau 跑   4. bìng 冰   pìng 拼（盤）
2. bèi 卑   pèi 披   5. bok 搏   pok 撲
3. bài 跛   pài 批

'g' and 'k'   *(Track 012)*

1. gāt 吉   kāt 咳   4. gèui 居   kèui 區
2. gèung 薑   kèuhng 強   5. géi 幾   kéi（屋）企
3. gìng 經   kìng 傾

'd' and 't'   *(Track 013)*

1. dēng 釘   tēng 廳   4. dou 到   tou 套
2. diu 吊   tiu 跳   5. dung 凍   tung 痛
3. dyún 短   tyúhn 斷

'gw' and 'kw'   *(Track 014)*

1. gwóng 廣   kwong 鄺   4. gwok 國   kwok 擴
2. gwài 歸   kwài 規   5. gwà 瓜   kwà 跨
3. gwaan 慣   kwaang 逛

'j' and 'ch'   *(Track 015)*

1. jāp 汁   chāp 輯   4. jóu 早   chóu 草
2. jeung 醬   cheung 唱   5. jyun 轉   chyun 寸
3. jit 節   chit 切   6. jūk 捉   chūk 束

DIFFICULT INITIAL DRILLS

'y'   *(Track 016)*

1. yàu 休
2. yèhng 贏
3. yeuk 約
4. yèung 央
5. yeuih 銳
6. yeuhn 潤
7. yiu 要
8. yīn 煙
9. yúk 玉

'ng'   *(Track 017)*

1. ngàaih 捱
2. ngàuh 牛
3. ngàih 危
4. ngàhn 銀
5. ngohk 鱷
6. ngouh 傲
7. ngāam 啱
8. ngúng
9. ngáng

'n' and 'ng'   *(Track 018)*

1. noh 糯   ngoh 餓
2. ná 嬤   ngáh 雅
3. nok 諾   ngok 惡
4. nouh 怒   ngouh 傲
5. nám 諗   ngám 黯

SIMILAR FINIAL DRILLS

'aa' and 'a'   *(Track 019)*

1. chàai 猜   chài 妻
2. gáam 減   gám 感
3. māau 貓   māu 踎
4. wáan 玩   wán 搵
5. sàang 生   sàng 生(命)
6. saahp 烚   sahp 十
7. waaht 滑   waht 核
8. āak 握   āk 扼

'ing' and 'eng' *(Track 020)*

1. pìhng 瓶   pèhng 平
2. dīng 丁   dēng 釘
3. tīng 聽（日）tēng 廳
4. gíng 景   géng 頸

5. hìng 興（旺）hèng 輕
6. jíng 整   jéng 井
7. líhng（引）領 léhng（衣）領
8. sìng 升   sèng 腥

'ek' and 'ik' *(Track 021)*

1. sehk 石   sihk 食
2. tek 踢   tīk 剔
3. jehk 蓆   jihk 直

4. pek 劈   pīk 辟
5. chek 尺   chīk 戚

'eng', 'ing' and 'in' *(Track 022)*

1. jèng 精（叮） jìng 晶   jìn 煎
2. tēng 廳   tīng 聽（日） tīn 天
3. chéng 請   chíng 拯   chín 錢
4. yèhng 贏   yìhng 仍   yìhn 然
5. behng 病   bihng 並   bihn 便

'euk', 'uk' and 'ok' *(Track 023)*

1. dēuk 踩   dūk 督   dohk（量）度
2. geuk 腳   gūk 菊   gok 角
3. jeuhk 着   juhk 續   johk 昨
4. leuhk 略   luhk 六   lohk 落
5. yeuhk 藥   yuhk 肉   wohk 鑊
6. seuk 削   suhk 熟   sok 索

'ong', 'eng' and 'ung'   *(Track 024)*

1. hòng 康	hèung 香	hùng 空
2. gòng 剛	gèung 薑	gùng 工
3. kwòhng 狂	kèuhng 強	kùhng 窮
4. jong 壯	jeung 醬	jung 眾
5. lòhng 狼	lèuhng 涼	lùhng 龍
6. sòng 桑	sèung 雙	sùng 鬆
7. chóng 廠	chéung 腸	chúng 籠

'o' and 'ou'   *(Track 025)*

1. dò 多	dōu 都	4. jó 左	jóu 早
2. tóh 妥	tóuh 肚	5. cho 錯	chou 醋
3. go 個	gou 告		

'e' and 'ei'   *(Track 026)*

1. bē 啤（酒）	bèi 卑	4. dé 嗲	déi（質）地
2. péh	péih 被	5. mē 咩	mēi（第）尾
3. ké 茄	kéi（屋）企		

'it' and 'ik'   *(Track 027)*

1. jiht 截	jihk 直	4. dīt 啲（多）	dīk 的
2. yiht 熱	yihk 亦	5. miht 滅	mihk 覓
3. chit 切	chīk 戚		

'eut' and 'euk'   *(Track 028)*

1. chēut 出	cheuk 卓	3. leuht 律	leuhk 略
2. jēut 卒	jeuk 雀	4. sēut 恤	seuk 削

'eun' and 'eung' *(Track 029)*

1. yeuhn 潤	yeuhng 樣	4. jéun 準	jéung 獎
2. chēun 春	chēung 窗	5. dēun 敦	dēung
3. seun 信	seung 相		

'-n' and '-ng' *(Track 030)*

1. sàn 新	sàng 生(命)	5. jaahn 賺	jaahng
2. bàn 賓	bàng 崩	6. maahn 萬	maahng 孟
3. jàn 真	jàng 憎	7. gón 趕	góng 講
4. sàan 山	sàang 生	8. hòn 看(護)	hòng 康

TONE DRILLS *(Track 031)*

1. sìn-sàang 先生
   fàan-gùng 返工
   chà-sìu 叉燒

2. kìng-gái 傾偈
   Hèung-góng 香港
   chèun-gyún 春卷

3. tìn-hei 天氣
   jùng-yi 鍾意
   Yīng-gwok 英國

4. sīng-kèih 星期
   Jùng-wàahn 中環
   fàan làih 返嚟

5. tīng-máahn 聽晚
   gàai-síh 街市
   jyù-láuh 豬柳

6. yàn-waih 因為
   dò-jeh 多謝
   gàm-yah 今日

7. hóu-tìn 好天
   síu-sàm 小心
   jóu-chāan 早餐

8. dím-gáai 點解
   géi dím 幾點
   síu-jé 小姐

9. tái hei 睇戲
    gó go 嗰個
    jáu-dim 酒店

10. géi-sìh 幾時
    Gáu-lùhng 九龍
    jáu-làuh 酒樓

11. tái-háh 睇吓
    hó-yíh 可以
    só-yíh 所以

12. chéng mahn 請問
    jó-mihn 左面
    cháau faahn 炒飯

13. daap līp 搭軩
    gei-dāk 記得
    jyun wāan 轉彎

14. bou-jí 報紙
    taai-táai 太太
    dung séui 凍水

15. fong-ga 放假
    gwai sing 貴姓
    fan-gaau 瞓覺

16. m̀h-gòi 唔該
    hùhng-sīk 紅色
    yìh-gā 而家

17. mùhn-háu 門口
    làih-jó 嚟咗
    yùh-gwó 如果

18. chìh-dou 遲到
    sìhng-haak 乘客
    làih-gwo 嚟過

19. sìh-sìh 時時
    pìhng-sìh 平時
    tùhng-màaih 同埋

20. kàhm-máahn 琴晚
    pàhng-yáuh 朋友
    m̀h-máaih 唔買

21. tùhng-sih 同事
    chìhn-mihn 前面
    hàahng-louh 行路

22. máaih syù 買書
    Méih-sàm 美心
    léuhng màn 兩蚊

23. Néih hóu 你好
    ngóh gwú 我估
    máaih-dóu 買倒

24. ngáahn-fan 眼瞓
    láih-baai 禮拜
    ńgh chi 五次

25. náaih-chàh 奶茶
　　yáuh-sìh 有時
　　léuih-hàhng 旅行

26. yáuh móuh 有冇
　　máaih yéh 買嘢
　　móuh yéh 冇嘢

27. tóuh-ngoh 肚餓
　　néih-deih 你哋
　　kéuih-deih 佢哋

28. dihn-wá 電話
　　Yaht-bún 日本
　　deih-há 地下

29. sahp baat 十八
　　sihk aan 食晏
　　deih-tit 地鐵

30. yih sahp 二十
　　hauh-mihn 後面
　　dihn-sih 電視

Lesson 1

Number 0 to 99

(Track 032)

romanization	Chinese character	hand signs
1 yāt	一	
2 yih	二	
3 sàam	三	
4 sei	四	

romanization	Chinese character	hand signs
5 ńgh or ḿh	五	
6 luhk	六	
7 chāt	七	
8 baat	八	
9 gáu	九	
10 sahp	十	
0 lìhng	零	

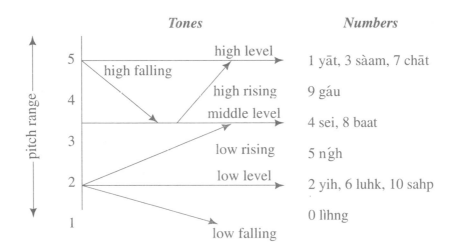

11 – 20   *(Track 033)*

11 sahp yāt   十一   16 sahp luhk 十六
12 sahp yih   十二   17 sahp chāt 十七
13 sahp sàam 十三   18 sahp baat 十八
14 sahp sei   十四   19 sahp gáu   十九
15 sahp ńgh   十五   20 yih sahp   二十

21 – 99   *(Track 034)*

20 yih sahp   二十 ..... 29 yih sahp gáu 二十九／yah gáu 廿九

30 sàam sahp   三十 ..... 39 sàam sahp gáu 三十九／sà-ah gáu 卅九

40 sei sahp   四十 ..... 49 sei sahp gáu／sei-ah gáu 四十九

50 ńgh sahp   五十 ..... 59 ńgh sahp gáu／ńgh-ah gáu 五十九

60 luhk sahp   六十 ..... 69 luhk sahp gáu／luhk-ah gáu 六十九

70 chāt sahp   七十 ..... 79 chāt sahp gáu／chāt-ah gáu 七十九

80 baat sahp   八十 ..... 89 baat sahp gáu／baat-ah gáu 八十九

90 gáu sahp   九十 ..... 99 gáu sahp gáu／gáu-ah gáu 九十九

EXERCISE

I.   Read the following numbers aloud

1. 19	6. 39	11. 35	16. 51
2. 64	7. 14	12. 76	17. 63
3. 87	8. 21	13. 49	18. 16
4. 93	9. 85	14. 28	19. 57
5. 74	10. 43	15. 72	20. 94

II.   Read the following calculations aloud, giving answers

1. 12 + 9 = 21

sahp yih gà gáu haih yah yāt

十　二　加　九　係　廿　一

2. 5 + 7

3. 8 + 35

4. 51 + 3

5. 13 + 29

6. 2 × 8 = 16

yih sìhng baat haih sahp luhk

二　乘　八　係　十　六

7. 9 × 7

8. 5 × 12

9. 8 × 11

10. 4 × 5

11. 97 – 5 = 92

gáu sahp chāt gáam ńgh haih

gáu sahp yih

九　十　七　減　五　係　九　十　二

12. 41 – 2

13. 76 – 4

14. 83 – 6

15. 58 – 1

> gáu sahp chāt is often said as gáu-ah chāt.

16. 63 ÷ 7 = 9

chāt chèuih luhk ah sàam haih gáu

七　除　六　十　三　係　九

17. 54 ÷ 9

18. 42 ÷ 3

19. 35 ÷ 5

20. 72 ÷ 8

III. Say your phone numbers

Néih dihn-wá géi-dō houh a?

你　電　話　幾　多　號　呀　?

What is your phone number?

Ngóh dihn-wá haih 93860959.

我　電　話　係　93860959。

My phone number is 93860959.

IV. Pair work

Student A forms a number hand sign. Student B says the number. For Cantonese hand signs, please refer to page 14 and 15.

V.   Matching pairs game.

Each student receives a number card and bears the numbers in mind. Once the game starts, go round the classroom, read the number to your classmates, and find out which classmate has the same number as yours. The student who found his partner sits down. The last to finish lose the game.

3048	3048	2569	2569
7152	7152	9130	9130
8673	8673	6285	6285

VI. Trump card games

1. Student draws out any card and read aloud.

    'A' = 1 & 'J' 'Q' 'K' = 0

2. Student A draws two trump cards and shows them to student B. Student B reads the numbers in Cantonese to student A. Student A repeats the numbers

in English.

'A' = 1   'J' 'Q' 'K' = 0

Example: '6' and '4' = 64   '6' and 'Q' = 60
          'J' and '6' = 06   'A' and '6' =16

3. This snap card game is called 'Kám mìhn tōi' 冚棉胎 (to cover the quilt).
Students sit in a circle in groups of two or more. A student holds a set of trump
cards and put them on the table one by one, while the whole group counts
from 0 to 13 repeatedly. When the card drawn is the same as the number
called by the group, snap on the pile immediately. The last to put his hand
on the cards loses the round and keeps the cards, then he has to put the cards
on the table while others count and snap.

'A' = 1   'J' = 11   'Q' = 12   'K' = 13

About telephone calls

Wrong number

Dá cho 打錯

Free telephone inquiry service

1081 in English
1083 in Cantonese
1088 in Mandarin

Emergency call

999 (for police, fire station and ambulance)

Taboos and popular beliefs about numbers

Lucky numbers

二　sounds the same as easy (yùhng-yih 容易).

三　sounds like lively, energetic (sàang-máahng 生猛).

八　sounds like prosperous and making money (faat 發 / faat-daaht 發達 / faat-chòih 發財).

九　sounds the same as long-lasting (chèuhng-gáu 長久).

Unlucky numbers

四　sounds like to die (séi 死). Fourteen and twenty four are not welcomed by Hong Kong people either. Fourteen sounds like 'saht séi' 「實死」 which means to die certainly. Twenty four sounds like easy to die (yih séi 易死). Many buildings in Hong Kong have no thirteenth (western unlucky number) and fourteenth (Cantonese unlucky number) floors.

七　is not welcomed by people, because this is a number which is used in Chinese funerals. Moreover, the pronunciation of 'chāt' sounds like a vulgar Cantonese word.

Lesson 2

Useful daily expressions

USEFUL EXPRESSIONS *(Track 035)*

1. Jóu-sàhn. 早晨。 — Good morning!

2. Néih hóu. 你好。 — Good day! / Nice to meet you.

There is no greeting similar to "Good afternoon" and "Good evening".

3. Bāai-baai. 拜拜。 — Bye!

4. Dāk. 得。 — Okay. / It's possible. / I can.

5. Haih a. 係呀。 — Yes, it is true. / You're right. / Yeah.

6. M̀h-gòi (saai). 唔該(晒)。 — Thank you (very much).

7. Dò-jeh (saai). 多謝(晒)。 — Thank you (very much) for your present, invitation, treat, expression of appreciation.

8. M̀h-sái. 唔使。 — There is no need to. (A reply to M̀h-gòi 唔該)

9. Faai-dī lā. 快啲啦。 — Faster please.

10. Dáng dáng. 等等。 — Please wait.

11. M̀h-hóu yi-sì. 唔好意思。 — Excuse me. / Sorry.

12. Móuh mahn-tàih. 冇問題。 — No problem.

M̀h-gòi 「唔該」 can also mean 'Excuse me' or 'Please' as in "please make way".

Sentence particles indicating mood　*(Track 036)*

1. Wa!　嘩！　　Wow! (Be excited or surprised)

2. Há?　吓？　　I can't hear you. / I can't believe it!

3. Oh!　哦！　　Oh I see. I understand.

4. Aai-ya!　哎吔！　Ouch! Oh no! / Too bad.

5. Wái?　喂？　　Hello (on the phone)

PRACTICE　*(Track 037)*

The following lines are about a person answering a phone call, read aloud, and translate the meaning.

1. Wái? Jóu-sàhn.　Néih hóu.　Haih a.
   喂？ 早 晨。 你 好。 係 呀。

2. Há?
   吓？

3. Aai-ya! M̀h-haih.
   哎 吔！ 唔 係。

4. Wa! Dāk m̀h dāk a?
   嘩！ 得 唔 得 呀？

5. M̀h-hóu yi-sì. M̀h-gòi dáng dáng.
   唔 好 意 思。 唔 該 等 等。

6. Haih, wái?
   係，喂？

7. Oh, hóu, hóu.　Dāk, dāk, dāk.　Móuh mahn-tàih.
   哦，好，好。 得，得，得。 冇 問 題。

8. M̀h-gòi saai. Bāai-baai.
   唔 該 晒。 拜 拜。

REVIEW EXERCISE

I.   What do you say when……

1. someone opens the door for you.

2. you greet someone at 8:00 a.m.

3. someone thanks you for your help.

4. ask people to hurry up.

5. ask the taxi driver to wait a moment.

6. your friend ask you to do a favor.

7. you want to make your way through.

8. you say good bye.

9. you receive a birthday present.

10. you meet someone for the first time.

11. you stepped on somebody.

12. you agree with what your friend said.

II.   Matching

1. Jóu-sàhn 早晨　　　　　•　　　　•　a. Please wait

2. Móuh mahn-tàih 冇問題 •　　　　•　b. Thank you very much

3. M̀h-gōi 唔該　　　　　•　　　　•　c. Nice to meet you

4. Dāk 得　　　　　　　•　　　　•　d. Okay

5. Néih hóu 你好　　　　•　　　　•　e. Good morning

6. Faai-dī lā 快啲啦　　　•　　　　•　f. Sorry

7. Dò-jeh saai 多謝晒　　•　　　　•　g. Please

8. M̀h sái 唔使　　　　　•　　　　•　h. No problem

9. Dáng dáng 等等　　　•　　　　•　i. There is no need to

10. M̀h-hóu yi-sì 唔好意思 •　　　　•　j. Faster please

Lesson 3

Turn left and stop please

A. *(Track 038)*

Ṁh-gòi, deih-tit jaahm hái bīn-douh a?
唔 該 ， 地 鐵 站 喺 邊 度 呀 ？
Excuse me, where is the MTR station?

> MTR 米
> Mass Transit Railway

Jihk heui, gāai-háu jyun jó jauh haih la.
直 去 ， 街 口 轉 左 就 係 喇 。
Go straight, turn left at the street junction, and there it is.

Ṁh-gòi-saai.
唔 該 晒 。
Thank you.

Ṁh-sái.
唔 使 。
You're welcome.

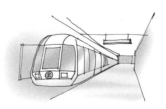

B. *(Track 039)*

Jóu-sàhn. Néih heui bīn-douh a?
早 晨 。 你 去 邊 度 呀 ？
Good morning. Where are you going?

Ngóh heui Wāan-jái. Néih nē?
我 去 灣 仔 。 你 呢 ？
I'm going to Wan Chai. What about you?

Ngóh heui Jùng-wàahn.
我 去 中 環 。
I'm going to Central.

Néih daap māt-yéh chè a?
你 搭 乜 嘢 車 呀 ？
What transport do you take?

Ngóh daap dīk-sí. Néih nē?
我 搭 的 士 。 你 呢 ？
I'll take a taxi. And you?

Ngóh daap deih-tit. Bāai-baai.
我 搭 地 鐵 。 拜 拜 。
I'll take the MTR. Bye.

Joi-gin.
再 見 。
See you again.

C. Take a Taxi *(Track 040)*

Heui bīn-douh a?
去 邊 度 呀 ？
Where do you want to go?

Ṁh-gòi heui Gáu-lùhng Jáu-dim.
唔 該 去 九 龍 酒 店 。
Please go to Kowloon Hotel.

Ṁh-hóu yi-sì, ngóh ṁh sīk heui.
唔 好 意 思 ， 我 唔 識 去 。
Sorry, I don't know how to go there.

Móuh mahn-tàih. Ngóh gaau néih hàahng.

有 問 題 。 我 教 你 行 。

No problem. I'll tell you how to go.

M̀h-gòi.

唔 該 。

Thank you.

Jihk heui, dāng-wái jyun jó, chìhn-mihn jyun yauh, nī-douh tìhng.

直 去 ， 燈 位 轉 左 ， 前 面 轉 右 ， 呢 度 停 。

Go straight, turn left after the traffic lights, turn right over there. Stop
here please.

USEFUL VOCABULARY   *(Track 041)*

1. heui 去	V :	go
2. jihk heui 直去	PH :	go straight
3. jyun jó 轉左	VO :	turn left
4. jyun yauh 轉右	VO :	turn right
5. nī-douh 呢度	PH :	here
6. gó-douh 嗰度	PH :	there
7. bīn-douh 邊度	QW :	where
8. tìhng 停	V :	stop

Drill

a) Nī-douh tìhng. 呢度停。   Stop here.
b) Chìhn-mihn tìhng. 前面停。   Stop there (in front).
c) Mùhn-háu tìhng. 門口停。   Stop at the entrance.
d) Jyun jó tìhng. 轉左停。   Turn left and stop.

9. yáuh lohk 有落	PH :	stop (used on minibuses only)

Drill

a) Gāai-háu yáuh lohk.   Stop at the street junction.
    街口有落。

b) Dāng-wái yáuh lohk.   Stop at the traffic lights.
    燈位有落。

c) Bā-sí jaahm yáuh lohk.   Stop at the bus stop.
    巴士站有落。

d) Deih-tit jaahm yáuh lohk.   Stop at the MTR station.
    地鐵站有落。

10. Jùng-wàahn 中環   PW : Central

11. Wāan-jái 灣仔   PW : Wan Chai

EXERCISE

I.   **Let one student be the taxi driver, another student be a passenger.**
     He would give instruction to the driver to go to the destination.

(Track 042)

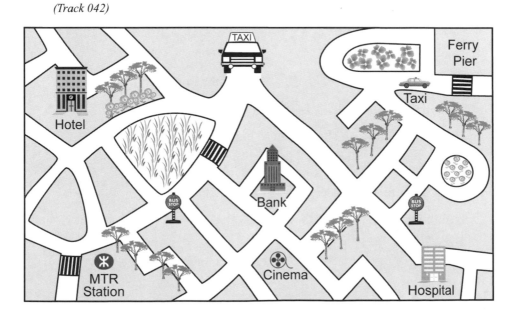

yī-yún 醫院	hospital
ngàhn-hòhng 銀行	bank
hei-yún 戲院	cincma
jáu-dim 酒店	hotel
deih-tit jaahm 地鐵站	MTR station
máh-tàuh 碼頭	ferry pier

II. How do you go to a place?   *(Track 043)*

Néih daap māt-yéh chè a ?
你　搭　乜　嘢　車　呀　？
What transport do you take?

Dím-yéung heui a ?
點　樣　去　呀　？
How do you get there?

Drill

Ngóh daap dīk-sí. 我搭的士。	I take a taxi.
Ngóh daap bā-sí. 我搭巴士。	I take a bus.
Ngóh daap síu-bā. 我搭小巴。	I take the minibus.
Ngóh daap deih-tit. 我搭地鐵。	I take the MTR (railway).
Ngóh daap dihn-chè. 我搭電車。	I take a tram.
Ngóh daap syùhn. 我搭船。	I take a ferry.
Ngóh daap fēi-gēi. 我搭飛機。	I take a plane.
Ngóh hàahng louh. 我行路。	I walk.
Ngóh jà-chè. 我揸車。	I drive.

(The tram is along the city on Hong Kong Island, it has a nick name called "dīng dīng 叮叮")

MTR announcements *(Track 044)*

1. Liht-chè jīk jēung dou-daaht.
   列 車 即 將 到 達 。
   The train is arriving.

2. Chéng maht kaau-gahn yuht-tòih mohk-mùhn.
   請 勿 靠 近 月 台 幕 門 。
   Please stand back from the platform screen doors.

3. Chéng síu-sàm chè-mùhn.
   請 小 心 車 門 。
   Please stand back from the doors.

4. Chéng síu-sàm liht-chè yúh yuht-tòih gāan hūng-kwīk.
   請 小 心 列 車 與 月 台 間 空 隙 。
   Please mind the gap between the tain and platform.

5. Chéng gàn-āak fū-sáu.
   請 緊 握 扶 手 。
   Please hold the handrail.

6. Hah yāt jaahm Jūng-wāan.
   下 一 站 中 環 。
   Next station, Central.

7. Sìhng-haak hó jyun sìhng Chyùhn-wāan Sin, Dūng-chūng Sin kahp Gēi-chèuhng Faai-sin.
   乘 客 可 轉 乘 荃 灣 線 、 東 涌 線 及
   機 場 快 線 。
   Interchange station for the Tsuen Wan Line, Tung Chung Line and Airport Express.

8. Jó-bīn chè-mùhn jēung-wúih dá-hói.
   左 邊 車 門 將 會 打 開 。
   Doors will open on the left.

Lesson 4

What time is it?

TELLING TIME

Clock Time   *(Track 045)*

Yìh-gā géi-(dō) dím a?
而 家 幾 多 點 呀 ?
What time is it now?

12:00   sahp-yih-dím (-jūng)
        十 二 點（鐘）

2:05   léuhng-dím-yāt
       兩 點 一

9:10   gáu-dím-yih
       九 點 二

4:15   sei-dím-sàam
       四 點 三

6:20 luhk-dím-sei
六點四

3:25 sàam-dím-ńgh
三點五

10:30 sahp-dím-bun
十點半

5:35 ńgh-dím-chāt
五點七

7:40 chāt-dím-baat
七點八

11:45 sahp-yāt-dím-gáu
十一點九

4:50 sei-dím-sahp
四點十

1:55 yāt-dím-sahp-yāt
一點十一

PRACTICE

I.   Translate the time into English

1. sei-dím-gáu 四點九
2. sahp-yih-dím-sàam 十二點三
3. nǵh-dím-bun 五點半
4. léuhng-dím-sahp 兩點十
5. baat-dím-chāt 八點七

II.   Tell the time in Cantonese

1. 5:25	6. 11:10	11. 8:14
2. 9:15	7. 3:59	12. 6:04
3. 1:20	8. 2:39	13. 10:40
4. 7:16	9. 12:45	14. 5:47
5. 6:35	10. 4:30	15. 11:55

III.   Student A tells student B a clock time. Student B draws it onto a clock face below. Take turns to practice.

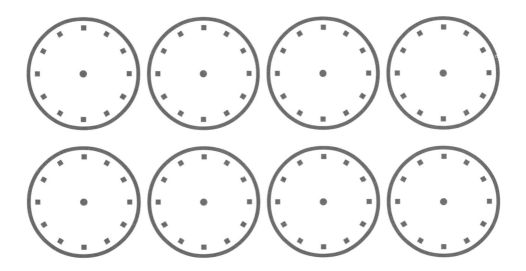

Day   *(Track 046)*

kàhm-yaht 琴日（噚日）/ chàhm yaht 噚日	yesterday
gām-yaht 今日	today
tīng-yaht 聽日	tomorrow

Monday to Sunday   *(Track 047)*

Sīng-kèih-géi a? 星期幾呀？	What day is it?
sīng-kèih-yāt 星期一 / láih-baai-yāt 禮拜一	Monday
sīng-kèih-yih 星期二 / láih-baai-yih 禮拜二	Tuesday
sīng-kèih-sāam 星期三 / láih-baai-sāam 禮拜三	Wednesday
sīng-kèih-sei 星期四 / láih-baai-sei 禮拜四	Thursday
sīng-kèih-ńgh 星期五 / láih-baai-ńgh 禮拜五	Friday
sīng-kèih-luhk 星期六 / láih-baai-luhk 禮拜六	Saturday
sīng-kèih-yaht 星期日 / láih-baai-yaht 禮拜日	Sunday

Date   *(Track 048)*

Géi(-dō) yuht géi(-dō) houh a?

幾 （多） 月 幾 多 號 呀 ？

What date is it?

Month

yāt-yuht 一月	January
yih-yuht 二月	February
sàam-yuht 三月	March
sei-yuht 四月	April
ńgh-yuht 五月	May
luhk-yuht 六月	June
chāt-yuht 七月	July

baat-yuht 八月   August

gáu-yuht 九月   September

sahp-yuht 十月   October

sahp-yāt-yuht 十一月   November

sahp-yih-yuht 十二月   December

EXERCISE

I.   Say the following time   *(Track 049)*

Example: 1:00 on 31st August, Tuesday

Baat-yuht sàam-sahp-yāt houh, sīng-kèih-yih, yāt dím

八 月 三 十 一 號 、 星 期 二 、 一 點

1. 25th December, Thursday

2. 30th July, Monday

3. 4th February, Friday

4. 16th April, Saturday

5. 27th November, Wednesday, 2:00

6. 12th September, Sunday, 1:45

7. 9th June, Tuesday, 10:30

8. 8th May, Monday, 6:25

II. Answer the questions. *(Track 050)*

1. Yìh-gā géi dím a?
   而 家 幾 點 呀 ?

2. Gàm-yaht haih sīng-kèih-géi a?
   今 日 係 星 期 幾 呀 ?

3. Sīng-kèih-yāt haih géi-dō houh a?
   星 期 一 係 幾 多 號 呀 ?

4. Tīng-yaht haih géi yuht géi houh a?
   聽 日 係 幾 月 幾 號 呀 ?

5. Gàm-yaht haih géi-dō yuht géi-dō houh a?
   今 日 係 幾 多 月 幾 多 號 呀 ?

6. Sīng-kèih-luhk haih géi-dō houh a?
   星 期 六 係 幾 多 號 呀 ?

7. Kàhm-yaht haih sīng-kèih-géi a?
   琴 日 係 星 期 幾 呀 ?

8. Chāt-yuht yih sahp sei houh haih sīng-kèih-géi a?
   七 月 二 十 四 號 係 星 期 幾 呀 ?

III. Answer the questions in Cantonese.

1. What time do you get up?

2. What time do you have lunch?

3. What time did you go home on Wednesday?

4. What time did you go to bed yesterday?

5. When did you come to Hong Kong?

6. When is Christmas?

7. When and what time was your first Chinese class?

8. When is your birthday?

Lesson 5

He is my friend

CONVERSATION

A. Two people meet for the first time. *(Track 051)*

Néih hóu. Ngóh haih Wòhng Gwok-gèi.
你 好 。 我 係 黃 國 基 。

Nī-go haih ngóh kāat-pín.
呢 個 係 我 卡 片 。
Nice to meet you. I am Wong Kwok Kei.
This is my business card.

> "ngóh kāat-pín" is short for "ngóh ge kāat-pín"

Dò-jeh. Ngóh haih Chàhn Mìhng-sī.
多 謝 。 我 係 陳 明 詩 。
Thank you. My name is Chan Ming Si.

Chàhn síu-jé, néih hái bīn-douh làih ga?
陳 小 姐 ， 你 喺 邊 度 嚟 㗎 ？
Miss Chan, where are you from?

Ngóh hái Yīng-gwok làih.
我 喺 英 國 嚟 。
I am from U.K.

B.   Mr Wong and Miss Chan meet again in a party.   *(Track 052)*

Wòhng sàang, hóu noih móuh gin.

黃 生 ， 好 耐 冇 見 。

Mr Wong, haven't seen you for a long time.

Néih hóu ma?

你 好 嗎 ？

How are you?

> "Wòhng sàang" is a short form of "Wòhng sìn-sàang"

Ngóh hóu hóu. Néih nē?

我 好 好 。 你 呢 ？

I am fine. And you?

Ngóh dōu hóu hóu.

我 都 好 好 。

I am fine too.

A Lìhng, nī-wái haih ngóh pàhng-yáuh Mìhng-sī.

阿 玲 ， 呢 位 係 我 朋 友 明 詩 。

(*Mr Chan turn to his wife.*) Ling, this is my friend, Ming Si.

Kéuih haih ngóh taai-táai, A Lìhng.

佢 係 我 太 太 ， 阿 玲 。

(*Then he turn to Ming Si.*) She is my wife, Ling.

> "ngóh taat-táai" is a short form of "ngóh ge taai-táai"

Wòhng táai, néih hóu.

黃 太 ， 你 好 。

Mrs. Wong, nice to meet you.

> "Wòhng táai" is a short form of "Wòhng taat-táai"

Mìhng-sī, néih hóu.

明 詩 ， 你 好 。

Ming Si, nice to meet you.

VOCABULARY   *(Track 053)*

1. ngóh 我   PN : I; me

2. néih or léih 你   PN : you

3. kéuih 佢   PN : he; him; she; her; it

4. ngóh-deih 我哋   PN : we, us

5. néih-deih or léih-deih 你哋   PN : you (plural)

6. kéuih-deih 佢哋   PN : they, them

7. sìn-sàang 先生   N : Mr; husband; teacher
    eg. Chàhn (sìn)-sàang 陳(先)生 : Mr Chan

8. síu-jé 小姐   N : Miss
    eg. Wòhng síu-jé 黃小姐 : Miss Wong

9. taai-táai 太太   N : wife, married woman, Mrs
    eg. Chàhn (taai)-táai 陳(太)太 : Mrs Chan

10. pàhng-yáuh 朋友   N : friend

11. tùhng-sih 同事   N : colleague

12. kāat-pín 卡(咭)片   N : business card

13. dihn-wá 電話   N : telephone

14. ge 嘅   P : indicating modification

15. go 個   M : used for counting people and
                                                  many other objects

16. wái 位   M : a polite form to count people

17. ga 架   M : used for counting vehicle,
                                                  machinc, etc.

18. dī 啲   M : indicating plural form or
                                                  uncountable

19. nī 呢	SP : this
eg. nī-go 呢個 : this one nī-dī 呢啲 : these	
20. gó 嗰	SP : that
eg. gó-go 嗰個 : that one gó-dī 嗰啲 : those	
21. bīn 邊	SP : used with measure to become which, who, whom, where
eg. bīn-go 邊個: which one; who bīn-dī 邊啲 : which of these	
22. haih 係	V : equal; verb to be
23. m̀h 唔	P : not

SENTENCE PATTERNS

A. Modifying a noun *(Track 054)*

☞ ＿＿＿ (＋ ge/ dī) ＋ noun : noun of ＿＿＿ , noun's ＿＿＿
＿＿＿ (＋ 嘅/啲) ＋ 名詞

eg. Ngóh ge pàhng-yáuh 我嘅朋友 : My friend(s)

Ngóh dī pàhng-yáuh 我啲朋友 : My friends

1. Ngóh ge taai-táai 我嘅太太   My wife

2. Kéuih ge dihn-wá 佢嘅電話   His (or her) telephone

3. Pàhng-yáuh ge pàhng-yáuh
朋友嘅朋友   Friend's friend(s)

4. A Lìhng ge sìn-sàang 阿玲嘅先生   The husband/teacher of Ling

5. Néih dī tùhng-sih 你啲同事   Your colleagues

6. Kéuih-deih dī chē 佢哋啲車   Their cars

7. Chàhn táai dī pàhng-yáuh   Mrs Chan's friends
    陳太啲朋友

8. Kéuih taai-táai 佢太太   His wife

9. Néih pàhng-yáuh 你朋友   Your friend(s)

10. Ngóh kāat-pín 我卡片   My business card

B. Specifying people or objects   *(Track 055)*

☞ Specifier + measure + noun 指定詞＋量詞＋名詞

eg. Nī-go pàhng-yáuh 呢個朋友   : this friend

Gó-go pàhng-yáuh 嗰個朋友   : that friend

Nī-dī pàhng-yáuh 呢啲朋友   : these friends

Gó-dī pàhng-yáuh 嗰啲朋友   : those friends

Bīn-go pàhng-yáuh 邊個朋友   : which friend

Bīn-dī pàhng-yáuh 邊啲朋友   : which group of friends

1. Nī-dī tùhng-sih 呢啲同事   These colleagues

2. Gó-wái taai-táai 嗰位太太   That married woman

3. Bīn-ga dīk-sí 邊架的士   Which taxi?

4. Nī-wái síu-jé 呢位小姐   This young lady

5. Gó-go kāat-pín 嗰個卡片   That business card

6. Nī-go dihn-wá 呢個電話   This telephone

PRACTICE

Choose the correct answer

1. She is your wife.

   Kéuih haih néih _____ taai-táai.

   佢 係 你_____ 太 太 。

   a) ge 嘅
   b) dī 啲
   c) bīn 邊

2. His colleague is my friend.

   Kéuih _____ tùhng-sih haih ngóh pàhng-yáuh.

   佢 _____ 同 事 係 我 朋 友。

   a) ngóh 我
   b) nothing
   c) dī 啲

3. My friends are late.

   Ngóh _____ pàhng-yáuh chìh-dou.

   我_____ 朋 友 遲 到 。

   a) haih 係
   b) go 個
   c) ge 嘅

4. That colleague's surname is Wong.

   Gó _____ tùhng-sih sing Wòhng.

   嗰_____ 同 事 姓 黃 。

   a) nothing
   b) go 個
   c) dī 啲

5. This is our boss.

   Nī- _____ haih ngóh-deih bō-sí.

   呢_____ 係 我 哋 波 士 。

   a) wái 位
   b) ge 嘅
   c) ngóh 我

6. He is not my husband.

   Kéuih m̀h-haih ngóh _____ sìn-sàang.

   佢 唔 係 我_____ 先 生 。

   a) nothing
   b) dī 啲
   c) deih 哋

7. I am waiting for my wife.

   Ngóh dáng ngóh _____ taai-táai.

   我 等 我_____ 太 太 。

   a) kéuih 佢
   b) dī 啲
   c) ge 嘅

8. His/Her phone number is 23460595   a) nothing

    Kéuih _____ dihn-wá haih 23460595.   b) néih 你

    佢 _____ 電 話 係 23460595。   c) bīn-go 邊個

C. Verb to be : 'haih' 係 *(Track 056)*

Affirmative statement

☞ Noun 1 + haih + Noun 2   Noun 1 = Noun 2
名詞 1 ＋ 係 ＋ 名詞 2

eg. Kéuih haih Chàhn sìn-sàang.
佢 係 陳 先 生 。
He is Mr Chan.

Negative statement

☞ Noun 1 + m̀h haih + Noun 2　Noun 1 ≠ Noun 2
名詞 1 ＋ 唔係 ＋ 名詞 2

eg. Kéuih m̀h-haih Chàhn sìn-sàang.
佢 唔 係 陳 先 生 。
He is not Mr Chan.

Question form

☞ Noun 1 + haih m̀h-haih + Noun 2 + a?
名詞 1 ＋ 係唔係 ＋ 名詞 2 ＋ 呀 ？

eg. Kéuih haih m̀h-haih Chàhn sìn-sàang a?
佢 係 唔 係 陳 先 生 呀 ？
Is he Mr Chan?
Answer: Haih. / M̀h-haih. 係 。/ 唔 係 。
Yes. / No.

1. Ngóh haih Wòhng Gwok-gēi.
   我 係 黃 國 基 。

2. Kéuih haih Chàhn sàang ge pàhng-yáuh.
   佢 係 陳 生 嘅 朋 友 。

3. Nī-go m̀h-haih kéuih dihn-wá.
   呢 個 唔 係 佢 電 話 。

4. Wòhng táai m̀h-haih ngóh pàhng-yáuh.
   黃 太 唔 係 我 朋 友 。

5. Kéuih haih ngóh taai-táai.
   佢 係 我 太 太 。

6. Chàhn sàang haih kéuih pàhng-yáuh,
   m̀h-haih kéuih sìn-sàang.

   陳 生 係 佢 朋 友 ，
   唔 係 佢 先 生 。

   > "sìn-sàang" can refer to someone's husband or teacher

7. Kéuih-deih haih m̀h-haih néih tùhng-sih a?
   佢 哋 係 唔 係 你 同 事 呀 ?

8. Kéuih haih m̀h-haih Wòhng sìn-sàang ge pàhng-yáuh a?
   佢 係 唔 係 黃 先 生 嘅 朋 友 呀 ?

9. Mìhng-sī m̀h-haih ngóh pàhng-yáuh.
   明 詩 唔 係 我 朋 友 。

10. Nī-go haih ngóh kāat-pín.
    呢 個 係 我 卡 片 。

PYRAMID DRILLS   *(Track 057)*

Chàhn Gà-mìhng
陳 家 明

haih Chàhn Gà-mìhng
係 陳 家 明

Kéuih haih Chàhn Gà-mìhng
佢 係 陳 家 明

Kéuih m̀h-haih Chàhn Gà-mìhng

佢 唔 係 陳 家 明

Kéuih m̀h-haih néih pàhng-yáuh Chàhn Gà-mìhng

佢 唔 係 你 朋 友 陳 家 明

Kéuih haih m̀h-haih néih pàhng-yáuh Chàhn Gà-mìhng a?

佢 係 唔 係 你 朋 友 陳 家 明 呀 ？

SUBSTITUTION DRILLS   *(Track 058)*

1. Kéuih haih <u>Wòhng sìn-sàang</u>. 佢 係 黃 先 生 。

   a) ngóh taai-táai   c) Chàhn Mìhng-sī

      我太太   陳明詩

   b) Wòhng síu-jé ge pàhng-yáuh d) Chàhn táai ge tùhng-sih

      黃小姐嘅朋友   陳太嘅同事

2. Néih haih m̀h-haih <u>kéuih tùhng-sih</u> a? 你 係 唔 係 佢 同 事 呀？

   a) Wòhng Gwok-gēi 黃國基   c) Wòhng síu-jé 黃小姐

   b) kéuih pàhng-yáuh 佢朋友   d) Chàhn táai 陳太

REVIEW EXERCISE

I.   Fill in the blanks

1. Ngóh _____ Wòhng Mìhng-sī.

   我 _____ 黃 明 詩 。

2. Kéuih haih néih _____.

   佢 係 你 _____ 。

3. Hòh sìn-sàang _____ -haih ngóh tùhng-sih.

   何　先　生　_____　係　我　同　事　。

4. Chàhn táai _____ néih pàhng-yáuh _____ ?

   陳　太　_____　你　朋　友　_____　?

5. Ngóh haih _____ .

   我　係　_____　。

II. Translation

1. Are they Mr Ho's colleagues? (Ho = Hòh 何).

2. Is she your wife?

3. Miss Chan is not the friend of Mrs Wong.

4. She is their friend, not my colleague.

5. Is your phone (number) 36275600?

6. Sorry, this is not Mr Chan's business card.

7. Who are you?

8. He is my teacher.

III. Answer the questions.   *(Track 059)*

1. Gàm-yaht haih m̀h-haih sahp houh a?
   今　日　係　唔　係　十　號　呀　?

2. M̀h-gòi,　yìh-gā géi-dō dím a?
   唔　該　，　而　家　幾　多　點　呀　?

3. Kàhm-yaht haih géi-dō houh a?
   琴　日　係　幾　多　號　呀　?

4. Nī-go haih m̀h-haih néih dihn-wá a?
   呢　個　係　唔　係　你　電　話　呀　?

5. Jóu-sàhn. Néih heui bīn-douh a?
   早 晨 。 你 去 邊 度 呀 ？

6. Néih daap māt-yéh chē a?
   你 搭 乜 嘢 車 呀 ？

7. Chàhn sàang haih m̀h-haih néih pàhng-yáuh a?
   陳 生 係 唔 係 你 朋 友 呀 ？

8. Heui Jūng-wàahn daap māt-yéh chē a?
   去 中 環 搭 乜 嘢 車 呀 ？

9. Ngóh heui Wāan-Jái. Néih nē?
   我 去 灣 仔 。 你 呢 ？

10. (Dīk-sí) Hái bīn-douh tìhng a?
    （的 士） 喺 邊 度 停 呀 ？

11. Deih-tit jaahm hái bīn-douh a?
    地 鐵 站 喺 邊 度 呀 ？

12. Néih hái bīn-douh làih ga?
    你 喺 邊 度 嚟 㗎 ？

IV. Where are you from?   *(Track 060)*

Australia Ou-jāu 澳洲	Holland Hòh-lāan 荷蘭	Korea Hòhn-gwok 韓國
Canada Gā-nàh-daaih 加拿大	India Yan-douh 印度	Malaysia Máh-lòih-sāi-a 馬來西亞
China Jūng-gwok 中國	Indonesia Yan-nèih 印尼	New Zealand Náu-sāi-làahn 紐西蘭
Denmark Dāan-mahk 丹麥	Ireland Oi-yíh-làahn 愛爾蘭	Philippines Fēi-leuht bān 菲律賓
France Faat-gwok 法國	Italy Yi-daaih-leih 意大利	Russia Ngòh-lòh-sī 俄羅斯
Germany Dāk-gwok 德國	Japan Yaht-bún 日本	Scotland Sōu-gaak-làahn 蘇格蘭

| Singapore
Sān-ga-bō 新加坡 | Taiwan
Tòih-wāan 台灣 | United Kingdom
Yīng-gwok 英國 |
| Spain
Sāi-bāan-ngàh 西班牙 | Thailand
Taai-gwok 泰國 | U.S.A.
Méih-gwok 美國 |

LISTENING EXERCISE   (Track 061)

I.   Multiple Choice

1. Mrs Chan   _____

2. My colleague   _____

3. Their friend   _____

4. Your husband   _____

II.   Use the given information, give true and false to the statements on the CD.   (Track 062)

> Mr Chan is the colleague of Miss Ho and Mrs Lee.
>
> Mr Wong is the husband of Miss Ho.
>
> Mr Wong and the husband of Mrs Lee are friend.
>
> Ji-ming is the friend of Mr Chan.

Chan : Chàhn 陳   Ho : Hòh 何   Lee : Léih 李

Wong : Wòhng 王   Ji-ming : Ji-mìhng 志明

1. _____   3. _____   5. _____   7. _____

2. _____   4. _____   6. _____

Lesson 6

How much is this?

A. Buying a bag   *(Track 063)*

Ṁh-gòi, nī-go dói yáuh māt-yéh sīk a?
唔 該 ， 呢 個 袋 有 乜 嘢 色 呀 ？
Excuse me, what color does this bag comes in?

Yáuh hùhng-sīk, làahm-sīk, hāak-sīk.
有 紅 色 、 藍 色 、 黑 色 。
This bag comes in red, blue and black.

Ngóh jùng-yi làahm-sīk ge. Yáuh móuh daaih-dī ga ?
我 鍾 意 藍 色 嘅 。 有 冇 大 啲 㗎 ？
I like the blue one. Do you have a bigger one?

Yáuh. Néih tái-háh nī-go lā.
有 。 你 睇 吓 呢 個 啦 。
Yes. Please take a look at this.

Nī-go géi-dō chín a?
呢 個 幾 多 錢 呀 ？
How much is this?

Yāt baak mān, chāt ńgh jit, jit-jó chāt-sahp-ńgh mān.

一 百 蚊 ， 七 五 折 ， 折 咗 七 十 五 蚊 。

$100, 25% off, it is $75 after discount.

 Pèhng-dī lā. Chāt-sahp mān dāk lā.

平 啲 啦 。 七 十 蚊 得 啦 。

Cheaper? How about $70?

 Hóu lā. Dò-jeh saai.

好 啦 ， 多 謝 晒 。

Okay, thank you.

B. Buying clothes (Track 064)

 Ṁh-gòi, nī-gihn sāam yáuh móuh ngóh ge sāai-sí a?

唔 該 ， 呢 件 衫 有 冇 我 嘅 晒 士 呀 ？

Excuse me, does this shirt comes in my size?

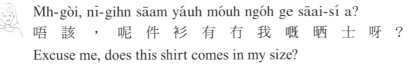 Yáuh, néih si-háh nī gihn lā.

有 ， 你 試 吓 呢 件 啦 。

Yes, please try this on.

 Ṁh-gòi, yáuh móuh sai-dī ga?

唔 該 ， 有 冇 細 啲 㗎 ？

Excuse me, do you have a smaller one?

Nī-gihn dāk ga la, ṁh-sái sai-dī lā.

呢 件 得 㗎 喇 ， 唔 使 細 啲 啦 。

This is OK. You don't need a smaller one.

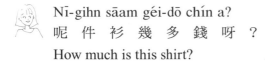 Nī-gihn sāam géi-dō chín a?

呢 件 衫 幾 多 錢 呀 ？

How much is this shirt?

 Sāam baak mān.

三 百 蚊 。

$300.

Yáuh móuh jit a??
有 冇 折 呀 ？
Do you have a discount?

‘móuh 冇’ is the oppsite of ‘yáuh 有’. Don't say ‘m̀h-yáuh’.

Móuh jit wo, m̀h-hóu-yi-sī.
冇 折 喎 ， 唔 好 意 思 。
No discount, sorry.

Yáuh móuh sàn ga?
有 冇 新 㗎 ？
Do you have a new one?

Yáuh. Néih dáng dáng lā.
有 。 你 等 等 啦 。
Yes. Wait a moment please.

Ngóh béi kāat dāk m̀h-dāk a?
我 畀 卡 得 唔 得 呀 ？
Is it okay if I pay by credit card?

Dāk.
得 。
Yes.

kāat 卡 : the abbreviation of credit card ‘seun-yuhng kāat’ 信用卡.

VOCABULARY   *(Track 065)*

1.	yáuh 有	V : have; possess; exist
2.	móuh 冇	V : do not have; without
3.	chín 錢	N : money

eg. Géi(-dō) chín a? 幾(多)錢呀 ？ : How much is this?

4. jit 折   N : discount

   eg. gáu jit 九折 : 10% off

      chāt ńgh jit 七五折 : 25% off

      Géi-dō jit? 幾多折 : What's the discount?

5. sāam 衫   N : clothes

   eg. yāt gihn sāam 一件衫 : a piece of clothing

6. dói 袋   N : bag

   eg. yāt go dói 一個袋 : a bag

7. hóu 好   ADJ : fine; good

                                               ADV : very

8. daaih 大   ADJ : big; large

9. sai 細   ADJ : small

10. gwai 貴   ADJ : expensive

11. pèhng 平   ADJ : cheap

12. leng 靚   ADJ : beautiful, good looking;
                                               good quality

13. sàn 新   ADJ : new

14. dī 啲   ADV : a little more

SENTENCE PATTERNS

A.   Money

Cents and dollars   *(Track 066)*

10 cents	yāt hòuh(-jí) 一毫（子）
50 cents	ńgh hòuh(-jí) 五毫（子）
$1	yāt mān 一蚊
$2	léuhng mān 兩蚊

| $10 | sahp mān 十蚊 |
| $100 | yāt baak mān 一百蚊 |

Cents and dollars combined   *(Track 067)*

$1.20	go-yih 個二
$1.50	go-bun 個半
$7.50	chāt-go-bun 七個半
$2.20	léuhng-go-yih 兩個二
$2.40	léuhng-go-sei 兩個四
$6.90	luhk-go-gáu 六個九
$10.10	sahp-go-lìhng-yāt 十個零一
$20.50	yih-sahp-go-lìhng-ńgh 二十個零五
$24.80	yah-sei-go-baat 廿四個八
$40.20	sei-sahp-go-lìhng-yih 四十個零二

PRACTICE

I.   Read the following money terms

1. $26.70   5. $300   9. $0.50   13. $2.20

2. $65.20   6. $13.90   10. $23.20   14. $91.40

3. $99.80   7. $49.40   11. $89.10   15. $54.60

4. $58.30   8. $1.50   12. $200

II.   Listen and write down the amount of money   *(Track 068)*

1. _____   4. _____   7. _____   10. _____

2. _____   5. _____   8. _____

3. _____   6. _____   9. _____

B. Possession and existence : 'yáuh' 有 *(Track 069)*

☞ *Affirmative statement :*   yáuh + noun
                              有 ＋ 名詞

    eg. Yáuh jit.
         有 折 。 (There is a discount.)

☞ *Negative statement :*   móuh + noun
                              冇 ＋ 名詞

    eg. Móuh jit.
         冇 折 。 (There is no discount.)

☞ *Question form :*   yáuh móuh + noun + a?
                        有冇 ＋ 名詞 ＋ 呀？

    eg. Yáuh móuh jit a?
         有 冇 折 呀 ？ (Is there any discount?)

    Answer: Yáuh. / Móuh.
         有 。 / 冇 。 (Yes. / No.)

1. Ngóh yáuh kéuih pàhng-yáuh ge dihn-wá.
   我 有 佢 朋 友 嘅 電 話 。

2. Néih yáuh móuh sàam sahp mān a?
   你 有 冇 三 十 蚊 呀 ？

3. Yáuh móuh daaih-dī ga?
   有 冇 大 啲 㗎 ？

4. Nī-go yáuh géi-dō jit a?
   呢 個 有 幾 多 折 呀 ？

5. Kéuih móuh pàhng-yáuh.
   佢 冇 朋 友 。

6. Ngóh yáuh Chàhn sàang ge kāat-pín.
   我 有 陳 生 嘅 卡 片 。

7. Ngóh yáuh hāak-sīk ge dói.
　我　有　黑　色　嘅　袋　。

8. Nī-douh móuh síu-bā.
　呢　度　冇　小　巴　。

C.　A little more : 'dī' 啲　*(Track 070)*

☞　　Adjective + dī
　　　形容詞　+　啲
　　　eg.　gwai-dī
　　　　　貴　啲　。　　a little more expensive

1. Yáuh móuh hóu-dī ga?
　有　冇　好　啲　㗎　?

2. Yáuh móuh sai-dī ga?
　有　冇　細　啲　㗎　?

3. Pèhng-dī dāk m̀h-dāk a?
　平　啲　得　唔　得　呀　?

4. Nī-go sàn-dī.
　呢　個　新　啲　。

5. Ngóh ge pàhng-yáuh leng-dī.
　我　嘅　朋　友　靚　啲　。

6. Bīn-go gwai-dī a?
　邊　個　貴　啲　呀　?

D.　Colour　*(Track 071)*

1. hāak-sīk 黑色　　　　　black

2. baahk-sīk 白色　　　　　white

3. hùhng-sīk 紅色   red

4. wòhng-sīk 黃色   yellow

5. làahm-sīk 藍色   blue

6. luhk-sīk 綠色   green

7. cháang-sīk 橙色   orange colour

8. jí-sīk 紫色   purple

9. (ga-)fē-sīk（咖）啡色   brown

10. fán-hùhng-sīk 粉紅色   pink

11. fùi-sīk 灰色   grey

12. gàm-sīk 金色   gold

13. ngàhn-sīk 銀色   silver

PRACTICE

What colour is this? :   Māt-yéh sīk a?
                            乜　嘢　色　呀　?

PYRAMID DRILLS   *(Track 072)*

1.
hāak-sīk
黑 色

yáuh hāak-sīk
有 黑 色

Nī-go yáuh hāak-sīk
呢 個 有 黑 色

Nī-go yáuh móuh hāak-sīk ga?
呢 個 有 冇 黑 色 㗎 ？

2.
sai-dī
細 啲

móuh sai-dī
冇 細 啲

yáuh móuh sai-dī ga?
有 冇 細 啲 㗎 ？

Hùhng-sīk ge yáuh móuh sai-dī ga?
紅 色 嘅 有 冇 細 啲 㗎 ？

SUBSTITUTION DRILLS   *(Track 073)*

1. Yáuh móuh daaih-dī ga? 有 冇 大 啲 㗎 ？
   a) sai 細   c) leng 靚
   b) pèhng 平   d) gwai 貴

2. Yáuh móuh kāat-pín a? 有 冇 卡 片 呀 ？
   a) dihn-wá 電話   c) jit 折
   b) pàhng-yáuh 朋友   d) luhk-sīk 綠色

REVIEW EXERCISE

Translation

1. Do you have a blue shirt?

2. Cheaper, please. How about $50?

3. This bag does not come in orange.

4. What colour is this?

5. The yellow one (costs) $75, the red one (costs) $38.

6. Does the pink one comes in a larger size?

7. Which one is newer?

LISTENING EXERCISE

I.   Listen to the following. If the English matches the Cantonese, write down Y, if not, write N.   *(Track 074)*

1. _____   3. _____   5. _____

2. _____   4. _____   6. _____

II. Listen to the dialogues and choose the correct answer.   *(Track 075)*

1. _____   3. _____   5. _____

2. _____   4. _____   6. _____

Lesson 7

Buying food and drink

A. Buying sandwich and drink   *(Track 076)*

Yāt go fó-téui dáan sāam-màhn-jih, yāt būi lìhng-mūng chàh, géi-dō chín a?

一 個 火 腿 蛋 三 文 治 ， 一 杯 檸 檬 茶 ， 幾 多 錢 呀 ？

A ham and egg sandwich, a cup of lemon tea, how much are they?

Yiht dihng dung lìhng-mūng chàh a?

熱 定 凍 檸 檬 茶 呀 ？

Hot or iced lemon tea?

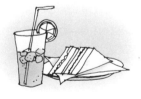

Dung líng chàh lā.

凍 檸 茶 啦 。

Iced lemon tea please.

Sāam-màhn-jih yih-sahp-yih-go-bun, líng chàh sahp-luhk mān, sà-ah-baat-go-bun lā.

三 文 治 二 十 二 個 半 ， 檸 茶 十 六 蚊 ， 卅 八 個 半 啦 。

Sandwich is $22.50, lemon tea $16, $38.50 please.

B. Stay here or take away? *(Track 077)*

Ngóh yiu léuhng go sā-léut.
我 要 兩 個 沙 律 。
May I have two salads please?

Yám māt-yéh a?
飲 乜 嘢 呀 ？
What do you want to drink?

Yāt gwun hó-lohk.
一 罐 可 樂 。
A can of coke please.

Hái douh sihk dihng līng-jáu a?
喺 度 食 定 拎 走 呀 ？
Stay here or take away?

Līng jáu, m̀h-gòi.
拎 走 ， 唔 該 。
Take away please.

Baat-sahp-ńgh mān lā.
八 十 五 蚊 啦 。
$85 please.

C. In a Hong Kong style cafe *(Track 078)*

Sìn-sàang yiu dī māt-yéh a?
先 生 要 啲 乜 嘢 呀 ？
What do you want?/What would you like?

Yáuh móuh chà-sìu faahn a?
有 冇 叉 燒 飯 呀 ？
Do you have BBQ pork with rice?

Yáuh.
有 。
Yes.

Yiu wún chà-sìu faahn lā.
要 碗 叉 燒 飯 啦 。
A bowl of BBQ pork with rice please.

> 'Yiu wún' is a short form of 'Yiu yāt wún 一碗'.

Yiu dī mè yám a?
要 啲 咩 飲 呀 ？
Do you want anything to drink?

> 'mè' = 'māt-yéh'
> '咩' = '乜嘢'

Béi būi ga-fē ngóh lā, m̀h-gòi.
畀 杯 咖 啡 我 啦 ， 唔 該 。
Please give me a cup of coffee.

Yiht dihng dung a?
熱 定 凍 呀 ？
Hot or cold?

Yiht ge.
熱 嘅 。
Hot.

D.   In the food court   *(Track 079)*

M̀h-gòi néih béi go B chāan ngóh līng-jáu, yám dung náaih-chàh.
唔 該 你 畀 個 B 餐 我 拎 走 ， 飲 凍 奶 茶 。
Please give me a set B, take away, the drink is iced tea with milk.

Hóu, dò-jeh.
好 ， 多 謝 。
Yes, thank you.

E. Buying fruit   *(Track 080)*

Sih-dō-bē-léi géi-dō chín a?

士 多 啤 梨 幾 多 錢 呀 ？

How much is the strawberry?

Sahp baat mān yāt hahp.

十 八 蚊 一 盒 。

Each box is $18.

Cháang nē?

橙 呢 ？

What about the oranges?

Cháang sahp mān sàam go.

橙 十 蚊 三 個 。

Oranges are $10 for 3.

Nī-go sāi-gwā géi-dō chín a?

呢 個 西 瓜 幾 多 錢 呀 ？

How much is this water melon?

Sà-ah yih mān.

卅 二 蚊 。

It is $32.

M̀h-gōi ngóh yiu nī-go sāi-gwā, yāt hahp sih-dō-bē-léi tùhng luhk go cháang.

唔 該 我 要 呢 個 西 瓜 、 一 盒 士 多 啤 梨 同 六 個 橙 。

I want this water melon, a box of strawberry and 6 oranges.

Chāt sahp mān lā.

七 十 蚊 啦 。

$70 please.

VOCABULARY   *(Track 081)*

1. yiht 熱	ADJ : hot	
2. dung 凍	ADJ : cold	
3. lìhng-mūng-chàh or nìhng-mūng-chàh 檸檬茶	N : lemon tea	*short as 'líng chàh 檸茶'*
4. náaih-chàh or láaih-chàh 奶茶	N : tea with milk	
5. ga-fē 咖啡	N : coffee	
6. hó-lohk 可樂	N : coke	
7. chà-sìu faahn 叉燒飯	N : BBQ pork with rice	
8. sàam-màhn-jih 三文治	N : sandwich	
9. sā-léut 沙律	N : salad	
10. cháang 橙	N : orange	
11. sāi-gwā 西瓜	N : water melon	
12. sih-dō-bē-léi 士多啤梨	N : strawberry	
13. wún 碗	N : bowl	
14. būi 杯	N : cup, glass, mug	
15. gwun 罐	M : can	
16. hahp 盒	M : box	
17. yiu 要	V : want; need	
18. yám 飲	V : drink	
19. béi 畀	V : give	
20. līng-jáu 拎走	V : take away, carry out	*other ways to say take away: 'hàahng-gāai 行街/ ngoih-maaih 外賣'*
21. hái douh sihk 喺度食	PH : eat here	

SENTENCE PATTERNS

A.   Or: 'dihng' 定   *(Track 082)*

☞   Object 1 + dihng + Object 2 + a? 名詞1 + 定 + 名詞2 + 呀？
eg. Hái douh sihk dihng līng jáu a?
喺 度 食 定 拎 走 呀？
Eat here or take away?

1. Jyun jó dihng jyun yauh a?
   轉 左 定 轉 右 呀 ？

2. Yiht dihng dung lìhng-mūng chàh a?
   熱 定 凍 檸 檬 茶 呀 ？

3. Néih daap deih-tit dihng bā-sí a?
   你 搭 地 鐵 定 巴 士 呀 ？

4. Néih yám chàh dihng ga-fē a?
   你 飲 茶 定 咖 啡 呀 ？

5. Sīng-kèih-yāt dihng sīng-kèih-sei a?
   星 期 一 定 星 期 四 呀 ？

6. Néih yiu yāt wún dihng léuhng wún chà-sìu faahn a?
   你 要 一 碗 定 兩 碗 叉 燒 飯 呀 ？

PRACTICE

Translate and answer the questions

1. You are taking a taxi or a bus?

2. What do you want, hot or iced coffee?

3. What do you want, strawberry or orange?

4. February or September?

5. $2 or $20?

6. 3:00 or 3:30?

7. Are you going to Central or Wan Chai?

8. How many bowls of rice do you want? 10 or 12 bowls?

B.   Give : 'béi' 畀   *(Track 083)*

☞   Person A + béi + number + measure + object + Person B

人 A + 畀 + 數目 + 量詞 + 名詞 + 人 B

eg. Kéuih béi yāt būi hó-lohk ngóh.

佢 畀 一 杯 可 樂 我 。

He gave me a glass of coke.

1. M̀h-gòi néih béi go sàam-màhn-jih ngóh lā.
   唔 該 你 畀 個 三 文 治 我 啦 。

2. M̀h-gòi néih béi léuhng būi chàh kéuih lā.
   唔 該 你 畀 杯 茶 佢 啦 。

3. M̀h-gòi béi sàam hahp chà-sìu faahn ngóh-deih.
   唔 該 畀 三 盒 叉 燒 飯 我 哋 。

4. Bīn-go béi sahp mān néih a?
   邊 個 畀 十 蚊 你 呀 ？

5. Néih béi dī māt-yéh Wòhng síu-jé a?
   你 畀 啲 乜 嘢 黃 小 姐 呀 ？

6. Hòh táai béi go cháang bīn-go a?
   何 太 畀 個 橙 邊 個 呀 ？

PRACTICE

Translate the followings

1. I give you $85.

2. Please give me your phone.

3. What did your friend give you?

4. Who should I give this white one to?

5. Who will give me a cup of tea with milk?

REVIEW EXERCISE

I. Make up dialogues to order the following things

1. 3 hot coffee and 1 iced lemon tea, $54

2. 2 teas with milk and a sandwich, $32

3. 1 coffee take away, $27.50

4. 1 small coke and 1 salad, $58.50

5. 1 BBQ pork with rice, eat here, $30

II. Translation

1. I drink iced coffee.

2. I don't want rice.

3. Do you want a large or small coke?

4. Two sandwiches are $72.20.

5. How many salad do you want?

6. Please give him a glass of iced lemon tea.

7. How much are 3 oranges?

8. Five cups of hot lemon tea are $60.

9. Please give me your business card.

10. Who should I give this $20 to?

Food sihk-bán 食品 *(Track 084)*

mihn-bāau 麵包 bread; bun	syut-gōu 雪糕 ice cream
dō-sí 多士 toast	syùh-tíu 薯條 French fries
sàam-màhn-jih 三文治 sandwich	syùh-pín 薯片 potato chips
hon-bóu-bāau 漢堡包 hamburger	sauh-sī 壽司 sushi
sā-léut 沙律 salad	chà-sìu faahn 叉燒飯 BBQ pork with rice
daahn-tāat 蛋撻 egg tart	yùh-dáan fán 魚蛋粉 fishball w/ rice noodles
jyū-gwū-līk 朱古力 chocolate	wàhn-tān mihn 雲吞麵 wonton w/ noodles

Drink yám-bán 飲品 *(Track 085)*

séui 水 water	ngàuh-náaih 牛奶 milk
bē-jáu 啤酒 beer	jān-jyū náaih-chàh 珍珠奶茶 Bo ba milk tea
hó-lohk 可樂 Coke	yūn-yēung 鴛鴦 Mixed coffee and tea w/ milk
syut-bīk 雪碧 Sprite	hùhng-dáu-bīng 紅豆冰 Iced sweet red bean w/ milk
cháang jāp 橙汁 orange juice	

Fruit sāang-gwó 生果 *(Track 086)*

pìhng-gwó 蘋果 apple	laih-jī 荔枝 lychee
ngàuh-yàuh-gwó 牛油果 avocado	gām 柑 mandarin orange
hēung-jīu 香蕉 banana	mōng-gwó 芒果 mango
làahm-múi 藍莓 blue berry	cháang 橙 orange
chē-lèih-jí 車厘子 cherry	muhk-gwā 木瓜 papaya
fó-lùhng-gwó 火龍果 dragon fruit	tóu 桃 peach
làuh-lìhn 榴槤 durian	léi 梨 pear
tàih-jí 提子 grapes	bō-lòh 菠蘿 pineapple
sāi-yáu 西柚 grapefruit	hā-maht-gwā 哈蜜瓜 rock melon
maht-gwā 蜜瓜 honeydew melon	yèuhng-tóu 楊桃 star fruit
kèih-yih-gwó 奇異果 kiwi fruit	sih-dō-bē-léi 士多啤梨 strawberry
lùhng-ngáahn 龍眼 longan	sāi-gwā 西瓜 water melon

Lesson 8

What time do you go home?

Néih géi dím fàan-gùng ga?
你 幾 點 返 工 㗎 ？
What time do you go to work?

> 'géi dím' is a short form of 'géi-dō dím'.

Ngóh gáu-dím fàan-gùng.
我 九 點 返 工 。
I go to work at 9:00.

Néih géi-dō dím sihk faahn a?
你 幾 多 點 食 飯 呀 ？
What time do you have lunch?

Ngóh sahp-yih-dím-bun sihk faahn.
我 十 二 點 半 食 飯 。
I have lunch at 12:30.

Néih géi dím fàan ūk-kéi a?
你 幾 點 返 屋 企 呀 ？
What time do you go home?

Ngóh luhk-dím-sàam fàan ūk-kéi.
我 六 點 三 返 屋 企 。
I go home at 6:15.

VOCABULARY   *(Track 088)*

1.	sihk faahn 食飯	VO :	eat rice; have lunch or dinner
2.	fàan-gùng 返工	VO :	go to work
3.	fàan-ūk-kéi 返屋企	VO :	go home
4.	séuhng-tòhng 上堂	VO :	attend a class
5.	héi-sàn 起身	VO :	get up
6.	fan-gaau 瞓覺	VO :	sleep
7.	chēut heui 出去	PH :	go out
8.	jouh 做	V :	to do

    eg. jouh māt-yéh 做乜嘢 : what do you do?

SENTENCE PATTERNS

Subject + time + verb   *(Track 089)*

☞ Subject + point of time + verb
主語 + 時間詞 + 詞

    eg. Kéuih baat-dím fàan-gùng.
    佢 八 點 返 工 。
    He goes to work at 8:00.

☞ Subject + géi(-dō) dím + verb + a?
主語 + 幾(多)點 + 詞 + 呀?

    eg. Néih géi(-dō) dím fàan-gùng a?
    你 幾(多) 點 返 工 呀 ?
    What time do/will you go to work?

☞ Subject + géi(-dō) dím + verb + ga?
主語 ＋ 幾（多）點 ＋ 詞 ＋ 㗎？

eg. Néih géi(-dō) dím fàan-gùng ga?
你 幾 （多） 點 返 工 㗎？
What time do you usually go to work? /
What time did you go to work?

☞ Subject + point of time + jouh māt-yéh a?
主語 ＋ 時間詞 ＋ 做乜嘢呀？

eg. Néih ńgh dím jouh māt-yéh a?
你 五 點 做 乜 嘢 呀？
What do you do at 5:00?

1. Ngóh baat-dím-bun sihk faahn.
   我 八 點 半 食 飯 。

2. Kéuih taai-táai gáu-dím-sàam fàan-gùng.
   佢 太 太 九 點 三 返 工 。

3. Néih luhk-dím jouh māt-yéh a?
   你 六 點 做 乜 嘢 呀 ？

4. Ngóh tùhng-sih ńgh-dím-bun fàan ūk-kéi.
   我 同 事 五 點 半 返 屋 企 。

5. Ngóh-deih géi dím séuhng-tòhng a?
   我 哋 幾 點 上 堂 呀 ？

6. Ngóh sahp-yāt-dím fan-gaau.
   我 十 一 點 瞓 覺 。

7. Néih géi dím héi-sàn ga?
   你 幾 點 起 身 㗎 ？

8. Kéuih chāt-dím-gáu chēut heui.
   佢 七 點 九 出 去 。

9. Kéuih baat-dím-bun jouh māt-yéh a?
   佢 八 點 半 做 乜 嘢 呀 ？

10. Kéuih géi-dō dím sihk faahn a?
    佢 幾 多 點 食 飯 呀 ？

PRACTICE

Use two pens as hands of the clock, ask each other what time is it, and what each other is doing at that time.

What time is it? : Géi-dō dím a?
幾 多 點 呀 ？

What are you doing? : Néih jouh māt-yéh a?
你 做 乜 嘢 呀 ？

PYRAMID DRILLS   *(Track 090)*

fàan-gùng

返 工

baat-dím-bun fàan-gùng

八 點 半 返 工

Kéuih baat-dím-bun fàan-gùng.

佢 八 點 半 返 工 。

SUBSTITUTION DRILLS   *(Track 091)*

1. Néih géi-dō dím sihk faahn a?   你 幾 多 點 食 飯 呀 ？

   a) fàan ūk-kéi 返屋企   c) fàan-gùng 返工

   b) fan-gaau 瞓覺   d) séuhng-tòhng 上堂

2. Kéuih baat-dím fàan ūk-kéi.   佢 八 點 返 屋 企 。

   a) gáu-dím-bun 9:30   c) sàam-dím-sei 3:20

   b) chāt-dím-sàam 7:15   d) ńgh-dím-yih 5:10

REVIEW EXERCISE

Translation

1. What time will you go home?

2. I have lunch at 1:00.

3. What will your colleague do at 3:30?

4. What time does your friend attend a class?

5. He slept at 11:45.

6. They are not going out.

Use the given information below, listen to the CD and answer the questions.

7:00	get up
8:30	go out
8:30 – 8:50	take MTR
9:00 – 1:00	work
1:00 – 2:00	lunch
2:00 – 6:00	work
6:00 – 7:00	attend a class
7:00 – 7:30	take minibus
7:30	go home
8:00	dinner
11:00	sleep

1. _____   5. _____

2. _____   6. _____

3. _____   7. _____

4. _____   8. _____

Lesson 9

I am busy

A.   What do you want to eat?   *(Track 093)*

Yìh-gā géi dím a?
而 家 幾 點 呀 ？
What time is it?

Yāt-dím la. Ngóh-deih heui sihk aan lā.
一 點 喇 。 我 哋 去 食 晏 啦 。
It's one o'clock. Let's go for lunch.

Hóu a! Ngóh hóu tóuh-ngoh.
好 呀 ! 我 好 肚 餓 。
Good! I'm hungry.

Sihk māt-yéh a ?
食 乜 嘢 呀 ？
What do you want to eat?

Sihk wàhn-tàn mihn hóu m̀h hóu a?
食 雲 吞 麵 好 唔 好 呀 ？
Do you want to eat wonton with noodles?

"sihk aan 食晏" is short for "sihk aan-jau faahn 食晏晝飯" eat lunch

Hóu aak. Faai-dī hàahng lā.
好 呃 。 快 啲 行 啦 。
Good. Let's go quickly.

B.   Mr Chan talk to Mrs Wong.   *(Track 094)*

Néih géi dím jáu a?
你 幾 點 走 呀 ？
What time will you leave?

Ngóh luhk-dím jáu.
我 六 點 走 。
I'll leave at 6:00.

Ngóh-deih heui tái hei lā.
我 哋 去 睇 戲 啦 。
Let's go to see a movie.

M̀h-hóu la. Ngóh fàan ūk-kéi tùhng sìn-sàang sihk faahn.
唔 好 喇 。 我 返 屋 企 同 先 生 食 飯 。
That's not a good idea. I'll go home to have dinner with my husband.

C.   Mrs Ho asks Mr Wong why he is so tired   *(Track 095)*

Hóu gwuih a!
好 攰 呀 ！
I'm very tired!

Néih kàhm-máahn géi dím fan-gaau ga?
你 琴 晚 幾 點 瞓 覺 㗎 ？
What time did you sleep last night?

Ngóh kàhm-máahn léuhng-dím fan-gaau.
我 琴 晚 兩 點 瞓 覺 。
I slept at 2:00 last night.

Dím-gáai a?
點 解 呀 ？
Why?

Yàn-waih ngóh tái dihn-sih.
因 為 我 睇 電 視 。
It's because I watched TV.

READING   *(Track 096)*

Ngóh chāt-dím-bun héi-sān sihk jóu-chāan, baat-dím daap-chè fàan-gùng.
我 七 點 半 起 身 食 早 餐 ， 八 點 搭 車 返 工 。
I get up and have breakfast at 7:30, take a bus to work at 8:00.

Ngóh yāt-dím tùhng tùhng-sih sihk aan. Ngóh luhk-dím fàan ūk-kéi,
我 一 點 同 同 事 食 晏 。 我 六 點 返 屋 企 ，
I have lunch with colleagues at 1:00. I go home at 6:00,

yìhn-hauh tùhng taai-táai sihk-máahn-faahn. Sihk faahn jì-hauh, ngóh tái
然 後 同 太 太 食 晚 飯 。 食 飯 之 後 ， 我 睇
and then have dinner with my wife. After dinner, I watch

dihn-sih. Ngóh sahp-yāt-dím fan-gaau.
電 視 。 我 十 一 點 瞓 覺 。
TV. I sleep at 11:00.

VOCABULARY   *(Track 097)*

1. làih or lèih 嚟	V : come
2. jáu 走	V : leave, go away, run
3. daap-chè 搭車	VO : take a transport
4. tái dihn-sih 睇電視	VO : watch TV

5. tái hei 睇戲	N : see a movie
6. tùhng 同	CON : and; together with
7. yāt-chàih 一齊	ADV : together
8. dím-gáai 點解	QW : why
9. yàn-waih 因為	CON : because
10. géi 幾 + ADJ	ADV : quite
11. tóuh-ngoh 肚餓	ADJ : hungry
12. gwuih 攰	ADJ : tired
13. mòhng 忙	ADJ : busy
14. dāk-hàahn 得閒	ADJ : have free time

SENTENCE PATTERNS

A. Purpose   *(Track 098)*

☞ Describe actions in the sequence of how things happen

> *eg.* Ngóh daap dīk-sí fàan-gùng.
>
> 我 搭 的 士 返 工 。
>
> I take a taxi to work.

1. Ngóh fàan ūk-kéi tái dihn-sih.
   我 返 屋 企 睇 電 視 。

2. Ngóh-deih heui Jūng-wàahn tái hei lā.
   我 哋 去 中 環 睇 戲 啦 。

3. Ngóh daap síu-bā fàan-gùng.
   我 搭 小 巴 返 工 。

4. Néih-deih làih ngóh ūk-kéi sihk faahn lā.
   你 哋 嚟 我 屋 企 食 飯 啦 。

5. Chàhn sàang daap-chè heui Wāan-jái.
   陳 生 搭 車 去 灣 仔 。

6. Néih heui Jūng-wàahn jouh māt-yéh a?
   你 去 中 環 做 乜 嘢 呀 ？

B. And/with : 'tùhng' 同 *(Track 099)*

☞ 　*Affirmative statement*
　　noun 1 + tùhng + noun 2
　　名詞 1 ＋ 同 ＋ 名詞 2

　　eg. Ngóh tùhng taai-táai sihk faahn.
　　　我 同 太 太 食 飯 。
　　　I eat with my wife.

☞ 　*Negative statement*
　　noun 1 + m̀h-tùhng + noun 2
　　名詞 1 ＋ 唔同 ＋ 名詞 2

　　eg. Ngóh m̀h-tùhng taai-táai sihk faahn.
　　　我 唔 同 太 太 食 飯 。
　　　I don't eat with my wife.

☞ 　*Question form*
　　noun 1 + tùhng m̀h-tùhng + noun 2 + a?
　　名詞 1 ＋ 同唔同 ＋ 名詞 2 ＋ 呀 ？

　　eg. Néih tùhng m̀h-tùhng taai-táai sihk faahn a?
　　　你 同 唔 同 太 太 食 飯 呀 ？
　　　Do you eat with your wife?

　　Answer:　Tùhng. / M̀h-tùhng.
　　　　　　　同 。 / 唔 同 。　Yes. / No

☞   Person A + tùhng + bīn-go + verb + a?
人 A ＋ 同 ＋ 邊個 ＋ 詞 ＋ 呀？

eg. Néih tùhng bīn-go sihk faahn a?
你 同 邊 個 食 飯 呀 ？
Who do you eat with?

1. Ngóh tùhng pàhng-yáuh tái hei.
我 同 朋 友 睇 戲 。

2. Néih tùhng bīn-go làih ngóh ūk-kéi a?
你 同 邊 個 嚟 我 屋 企 呀 ？

3. Kéuih tùhng taai-táai fàan ūk-kéi.
佢 同 太 太 返 屋 企 。

4. Ngóh tùhng tùhng-sih yāt-dím séuhng-tòhng.
我 同 同 事 一 點 上 堂 。

5. Néih sìn-sàang tùhng-m̀h-tùhng néih sihk faahn a?
你 先 生 同 唔 同 你 食 飯 呀 ？

6. Néih tùhng-m̀h-tùhng ngóh heui yám ga-fē a?
你 同 唔 同 我 去 飲 咖 啡 呀 ？

7. Ngóh m̀h-tùhng kéuih daap dīk-sí.
我 唔 同 佢 搭 的 士 。

8. Ngóh hóu gwuih, m̀h-tùhng kéuih-deih chēut heui la.
我 好 劫 ， 唔 同 佢 哋 出 去 喇 。

PRACTICE

Translate the following questions then answer

1. Who do you have dinner with?

2. What time do you have lunch with Mr Lee?

3. What day will they have tea with friends?

4. Will you go to movie with Miss Wong?

5. What do you do with your colleague?

6. Where do you go with your friends?

C. Use of adjectives *(Track 100)*

☞ *High degree :*	hóu mòhng		
	好　忙		very busy
☞ *Medium :*	géi mòhng		
	幾　忙		quite busy
☞ *Low degree :*	m̀h-haih géi mòhng		
	唔　係　幾　忙		not very busy
	m̀h-mòhng		
	唔　忙		not busy
☞ *Question form :*	Néih mòhng m̀h-mòhng a ?		
	你　忙　唔　忙　呀？		Are you busy
	Néih dāk m̀h dāk-hàahn a?		
	你　得　唔　得　閒　呀？		Are you free?

1. Kéuih sihk faahn hóu faai.
   佢　食　飯　好　快　。

2. Néih-deih gwuih m̀h-gwuih a?
   你　哋　劫　唔　劫　呀？

3. Daap dihn-chē hóu pèhng.
   搭　電　車　好　平　。

4. Néih sīng-kèih-ńgh mòhng m̀h-mòhng a?
   你　星　期　五　忙　唔　忙　呀？

5. Kéuih-deih m̀h-dāk-hàahn.
   佢　哋　唔　得　閒　。

6. Kéuih ge pàhng-yáuh leng m̀h-leng a?
   佢 嘅 朋 友 靚 唔 靚 呀 ？

7. Ngóh hóu mòhng, m̀h-tùhng néih sihk faahn la.
   我 好 忙 ， 唔 同 你 食 飯 喇 。

8. Néih tóuh m̀h-tóuh-ngoh a?
   你 肚 唔 肚 餓 呀 ？

9. Nī-būi ga-fē m̀h-haih géi gwai.
   呢 杯 咖 啡 唔 係 幾 貴 。

10. Nī-ga dihn-sih hóu sān.
    呢 架 電 視 好 新 。

REVIEW FINAL PARTICLES

a 呀 :   exclamation; choice type question; question with question word(s)

ga 㗎 :   ge 嘅 + a 呀; asking habits; asking when action(s) has been completed; exclamation

àh 吖 :   I suppose?, equivalent to "haih m̀h haih a? 係唔係呀？"

lā 啦 :   please; let's

la 喇 :   indicating changes; already

1. Chat dím ____. Fàan ūk-kéi ____.
   七 點 ____ 。 返 屋 企 ____ 。
   It's already seven o'clock. Let's go home.

2. Ngóh-deih heui sihk faahn, néih m̀h-heui ____?
   我 哋 去 食 飯 ， 你 唔 去 ____ ？
   We are going to have dinner, and you are not going with us?

3. Ngóh hóu tóuh-ngóh. Heui sihk faahn ____ .
   我 好 肚 餓 。 去 食 飯 ____ 。
   I am hungry. Let's go for lunch.

4. Néih géi dím fàan-gùng ____ ?
   你 幾 點 返 工 ____ ?
   What time do you usually go to work?

5. Ngóh-deih tīng-yaht géi-dím séuhng-tòhng ____ ?
   我 哋 聽 日 幾 點 上 堂 ____ ?
   What time is our class tomorrow?

6. Ngóh yìh-gā chēut heui ____ .
   我 而 家 出 去 ____ 。
   I am going out now.

7. Ngóh-deih yāt-chàih daap-dīk-sí jáu ____ .
   我 哋 一 齊 搭 車 走 ____ 。
   Let's leave together by taxi.

8. Néih kàhm-máahn (*last night) géi dím fan-gaau ____ ?
   你 琴 晚 幾 點 瞓 覺 ____ ?
   What time did you go to bed last night?

PYRAMID DRILLS   *(Track 101)*

1.
sihk faahn
食 飯

fàan ūk-kéi sihk faahn
返 屋 企 食 飯

daap síu-bā fàan ūk-kéi sihk faahn
搭 小 巴 返 屋 企 食 飯

Ngóh daap síu-bā fàan ūk-kéi sihk faahn.
我 搭 小 巴 返 屋 企 食 飯 。

2.

Néih heui

你　去

Néih tùhng taai-táai heui

你　同　太　太　去

Néih m̀h-tùhng taai-táai heui

你　唔　同　太　太　去

Néih tùhng m̀h-tùhng taai-táai heui a?

你　同　唔　同　太　太　去　呀　？

SUBSTITUTION DRILLS　(Track 102)

1. Ngóh tùhng pàhng-yáuh sihk faahn. 我　同　朋　友　食　飯　。
   - a) tùhng-sih 同事
   - b) taai-táai 太太
   - c) Chàhn sàang 陳生
   - d) Wòhng síu-jé 黃小姐

2. Kéuih m̀h-haih géi tóuh-ngoh. 佢　唔　係　幾　肚　餓　。
   - a) gwuih 劫
   - b) dāk-hàahn 得閒
   - c) yiht 熱
   - d) mòhng 忙

REVIEW EXERCISE

I.　Rewrite the following sentences

1. fàan ūk-kéi / ngóh / gàm-yaht / daap dīk-sí
   返　屋　企　／　我　／　今　日　／　搭　的　士

2. sīng-kèih-sei / kéuih-deih / sihk faahn / yāt-dím
   星　期　四　／　佢　哋　／　食　飯　／　一　點

3. taai-táai / m̀h-tùhng / kéuih / chēut heui
   太　太　／　唔　同　／　佢　／　出　去

4. hóu / dāk-hàahn / ngóh / pàhng-yáuh

好 / 得 閒 / 我 / 朋 友

II. Fill in the blanks

1. Ngóh baat-dím-bun _____ .

我 八 點 半 _____ 。

2. Ngóh sahp-yih-dím _____ .

我 十 二 點 _____ 。

3. Ngóh tùhng _____ tái hei.

我 同 _____ 睇 戲 。

4. Néih _____ tùhng-sih sihk faahn a?

你_____ 同 事 食 飯 呀 ？

5. Kéuih _____ sìn-sàang _____ .

佢_____先 生 _____ 。

III. Translation

1. I go to work by bus at 8:45.

2. They came at 7:15, and then went home at 10:30.

3. I will not have lunch with my wife.

4. I am not busy on Friday.

5. He is very tired.

6. Who do you have dinner with?

7. I'm going home now.

8. I go out with my friends on Saturday.

IV.　Ask and answer the questions

1. (gwai 貴)

Bīn gihn sāam gwai-dī a?　Géi chín a?
邊 件 衫 貴 啲 呀 ？ 幾 錢 呀 ？

2. (daaih 大)

Bīn-go dói daaih-dī a?
邊 個 袋 大 啲 呀 ？

3. (pèhng 平)

Bīn-go būi pèhng-dī a?　Gó-go būi géi chín a?
邊 個 杯 平 啲 呀 ？ 嗰 個 杯 幾 錢 呀 ？

4. (sàn 新)

Bīn-go sàn-dī a?
邊 個 新 啲 呀 ？

5. (leng 靚)

Bīn-go leng-dī a?
邊 個 靚 啲 呀 ？

6. (mòhng 忙)

Bīn-go mòhng-dī a?
邊 個 忙 啲 呀 ？

7. (gwuih 劼)

Bīn-go gwuih-dī a?
邊　個　劼　啲　呀　？

8. (sai 細)

Māt-yéh chè sai-dī a?
乜　嘢　車　細　啲　呀　？

LISTENING EXERCISE

I.   Listen to the sentences, choose the correct translation in Cantonese.

(Track 103)

1. It's now 7:30   _____

2. He and his colleague   _____

3. I go for lunch at 1:00 _____

4. Go home by car   _____

II. Listen to the dialogues and answer the questions. *(Track 104)*

1. _____   3. _____   5. _____

2. _____   4. _____   6. _____

III. Use the given information and answer the questions. *(Track 105)*

7:10	get up
8:00	take a taxi to work (with my wife)
9:00	start working
12:30	have lunch (with colleagues)
8:20	see a movie and have a drink (with friends)
10:45	go home
11:15	sleep

1. Néih géi dím héi-sān a?
   你 幾 點 起 身 呀 ？

2. Néih géi dím fan-gaau a?
   你 幾 點 瞓 覺 呀 ？

3. Néih tùhng bīn-go sihk faahn a?
   你 同 邊 個 食 飯 呀 ？

4. Néih tùhng taai-táai tái hei, haih m̀h-haih a?
   你 同 太 太 睇 戲 ， 係 唔 係 呀 ？

5. Néih sahp-dím-gáu fàan ūk-kéi àh?
   你 十 點 九 返 屋 企 吖 ？

6. Néih daap síu-bā fàan-gùng, haih m̀h-haih a?
   你 搭 小 巴 返 工 ， 係 唔 係 呀 ？

Lesson 10

Dim sum

CONVERSATION

A. At the reception *(Track 106)*

Sìn-sàang, géi wái a?
先 生 ， 幾 位 呀 ？
Sir, how many person?

Sei wái.
四 位 。
Four.

Gwai sing a?
貴 姓 呀 ？
May I know your name?

Ngóh sing Wòhng.
我 姓 黃 。
My name is Wong.

"sing 姓" = surname

(She gives Mr Wong a number card.)

Chéng dáng jahn.
請 等 陣 。
Please wait a moment.

(Ten minutes later)

45-houh Wòhng sàang, sei wái. M̀h-gòi nī-bihn.

４５ 號 黃 生 ， 四 位 。 唔 該 呢 邊 。

Number 45 Mr Wong. This way please.

B.   At the table   *(Track 107)*

Géi wái, yám mè chàh a?

幾 位 ， 飲 咩 茶 呀 ？

What kind of tea do you drink?

> géi wái 幾位 : a polite way for a waiter to address a group of people.

Yāt wùh bóu-léi,

yāt wùh gwán séui, m̀h-gòi.

一 壺 普 洱 ，

一 壺 滾 水 ， 唔 該 。

A pot of Pu'er tea, a pot of hot water please.

> mè 咩 : a variation of 'māt-yéh 乜嘢' (what)

Séung sihk dī māt-yéh a?

想 食 啲 乜 嘢 呀 ？

What would you like to eat?

Ngóh séung sihk hà-gáau.

我 想 食 蝦 餃 。

I want to eat shrimp dumplings.

Ngóh yiu chèun-gyún.

我 要 春 卷 。

I want spring rolls.

Hòh síu-jé jùng-yi sihk māt-yéh dím-sām a?

何 小 姐 鍾 意 食 乜 嘢 點 心 呀 ？

Miss Ho, what dim sum do you like to eat?

Sih-daahn lā.

是 但 啦 。

Up to you.

Sihk m̀h-sihk chà-sìu-bāau a?

食 唔 食 叉 燒 包 呀 ？

Do you like to eat BBQ pork bun?

Hóu aak.

好 呃 。

Yes.

(While eating dim sum.)

Nī-dī haih mè a?

呢 啲 係 咩 呀 ？

What are these?

Nī-dī haih sìu-máai.

呢 啲 係 燒 賣 。

These are pork dumplings.

Hòh síu-jé, néih jùng m̀h-jùng-yi yám chàh a?

何 小 姐 ， 你 鍾 唔 鍾 意 飲 茶 呀 ？

Miss Ho, do you like to eat dim sum?

Ngóh hóu jùng-yi yám chàh. Dī dím-sām hóu hóu-sihk.

我 好 鍾 意 飲 茶 。 啲 點 心 好 好 食 。

I love dim sum. These dim sum are delicious.

Sihk m̀h-sihk faahn a?

食 唔 食 飯 呀 ？

Do you want some rice?

Hóu aak. Yiu yāt-go Yèuhng-jàu cháau-faahn lā.

好 呃 。 要 一 個 揚 州 炒 飯 啦 。

Yes. Let's have a fried rice.

(After they finished the dim sum and fried rice.)

Báau meih a?

飽 未 呀 ？

Are you full?

Géi báau la.

幾 飽 喇 。

I'm quite full.

Ngóh séung sihk sài-máih-louh.

我 想 食 西 米 露 。

I want to have coconut milk with sago.

Ngóh dōu haih.

我 都 係 。

Me too.

(After they stop eating.)

Mh-gòi màaih-dāan.

唔 該 埋 單 。

Bill, please.

Dò-jeh sàam baak yāt sahp baat go gáu.

多 謝 三 百 一 十 八 個 九 。

$318.90 please.

Néih-deih sàu m̀h-sàu kāat ga?

你 哋 收 唔 收 卡 㗎 ？

Do you take credit card?

Sàu.

收 。

Yes.

Ṁh-gòi béi jèung dāan ngóh.

唐　該　畀　張　單　我　。

Please give me the bill / receipt.

Table manner

1. When someone pours tea for you, say 'ṁh-gòi' 唔該 and knock with the first two fingers on the table. This symbolises bowing to show thanks for his/her kindness.

2. When you want to refill the teapot, lift up the lid, put it aside and wait, or you can tell the waiter 'Ṁh-gòi chùng séui.' 唔該冲水 or 'Ṁh-gòi gà séui' 唔該加水.

3. Use the bowl and spoon for holding food. The plate is for holding bones and left-overs.

READING   *(Track 108)*

Gàm-yaht ngóh tùhng dī tùhng-sih heui yám chàh. Ngóh-deih yám bóu-léi,

今　日　我　同　啲　同　事　去　飲　茶　。　我　哋　飲　普　洱　,

Today I went for dim sum with my colleagues. We drank Pu'er tea,

sihk dím-sām tùhng cháau-faahn. Ngóh-deih dōu hóu báau. Léuhng dím,

食　點　心　同　炒　飯　。　我　哋　都　好　飽　。　兩　點　,

ate dim sum and fried rice. We were all very full. At two o'clock,

ngóh-deih màaih-dāan fàan gūng-sī. Hòh síu-jé hóu jùng-yi yám chàh.

我　哋　埋　單　返　公　司　。　何　小　姐　好　鍾　意　飲　茶　。

we got the bill and went back to the office. Miss Ho loves dim sum.

Ngóh-deih wah tīng-yaht dōu heui yám chàh. Kéuih hóu hòi-sàm.

我　哋　話　聽　日　都　去　飲　茶　。　佢　好　開　心　。

We said we would go for dim sum again tomorrow. She was very happy.

Chinese Tea   *(Track 109)*

1. bóu-léi/ póu-léi 普洱   Pu'er tea
2. hèung-pín 香片   Jasmine tea
3. tit-gwùn-yàm 鐵觀音   Iron Budha tea

Dim Sum   *(Track 110)*

1. hà-gáau 蝦餃   shrimp dumpling
2. sìu-máai 燒賣   pork dumpling
3. chèun-gyún 春卷   spring roll
4. chà-sìu-chéung 叉燒腸   rice roll with BBQ pork filling
5. hà-chéung 蝦腸   rice roll with shrimp filling
6. wuh-gok 芋角   fried mashed taro dumpling
7. chà-sìu-bāau 叉燒包   BBQ pork bun
8. chà-sìu-sōu 叉燒酥   BBQ pork pastry
9. gwun-tòng-gáau 灌湯餃   soup dumpling
10. fuhng-jáau 鳳爪   chicken feet (phoenix claw)
11. pàaih-gwāt 排骨   steamed spare rib
12. jàn-jyū-gāi 珍珠雞   glutinous rice dumpling with chicken filling
13. daahn-tāat 蛋撻   egg tart
14. hùhng-dáu-sā 紅豆沙   red bean sweet soup
15. sài-máih-louh 西米露   coconut milk with sago
16. mòng-gwó bou-dīn 芒果布甸   mango pudding
17. máh-lāai-gōu 馬拉糕   Malaysian sponge cake
18. chīn-chàhng-gōu 千層糕   Steamed layered custard cake
19. ja náaih-wòhng bāau 炸奶黃包   Fried custard bun

Rice and Noodles *(Track 111)*

1. Yèuhng-jàu cháau-faahn 揚州炒飯   Fried rice

2. Yuhk-sī cháau-mihn
   肉絲炒麵
   Crunchy noodles with shredded pork and bean sprouts

3. Sìng-jàu cháau-máih 星洲炒米   Singapore style fried vermicelli

4. Gòn-cháau ngàuh hó 乾炒牛河   Fried thick rice noodles with beef in soy sauce

VOCABULARY   *(Track 112)*

1. máaih 買	V : buy
eg. máaih-yéh 買嘢 : buy things; go shopping	
2. jùng-yi 鍾意	V/AV : like, like to
3. séung 想	AV : want to; wish to
4. wah 話	V : to say
5. séui 水	N : water
eg. gwán-séui 滾水 : boiled water, hot water	
dung-séui 凍水 : cold water	
bīng-séui 冰水 : ice water	
6. yám-chàh 飲茶	VO : drink tea; have tea and dim sum
7. dím-sām 點心	N : dim sum
8. hóu sihk 好食	ADJ : delicious; good to eat
9. báau 飽	ADJ : full (stomach)
10. hòi-sàm 開心	ADJ : happy
11. dōu 都	ADV : all, also

SENTENCE PATTERNS *(Track 113)*

A. Action at present or near future

> ***Affirmative statement***
>
> ☞ subject + verb 主詞 ＋ 動詞
>
> *eg.* Ngóh yám chàh.
>
> 我　飲　茶　。
>
> I drink tea.

> ***Negative statement***
>
> ☞ subject + m̀h + verb 主詞 ＋ 唔 ＋ 動詞
>
> *eg.* Ngóh m̀h-yám chàh.
>
> 我　唔　飲　茶　。
>
> I don't drink tea.

> ***Question form***
>
> ☞ subject + verb m̀h-verb + (noun +) a?
>
> 主詞 ＋ 動詞 唔-動詞 ＋（名詞 ＋）呀？
>
> *eg.* Néih yám m̀h-yám chàh a?
>
> 你　飲　唔　飲　茶　呀　？
>
> Do you drink tea?

1. Ngóh-deih m̀h tái-hei.
   我　哋　唔　睇　戲　。

2. Néih sihk m̀h-sihk dím-sām a?
   你　食　唔　食　點　心　呀　？

3. Néih tùhng-sih máaih m̀h-máaih chè a?
   你　同　事　買　唔　買　車　呀　？

4. Néih sīng-kèih-sei sèuhng m̀h séuhng-tòhng a?
   你 星 期 四 上 唔 上 堂 呀 ？

5. Néih yám m̀h-yám lìhng-mūng-chàh a?
   你 飲 唔 飲 檸 檬 茶 呀 ？

6. Kéuih pàhng-yáuh máaih nī-go hùhng-sīk ge.
   佢 朋 友 買 呢 個 紅 色 嘅 。

7. Ngóh m̀h-yiu gwán-séui.
   我 唔 要 滾 水 。

8. Kéuih-deih sīng-kèih-yaht chēut m̀h-chēut heui a?
   佢 哋 星 期 日 出 唔 出 去 呀 ？

9. Ngóh-deih yìh-gā heui yám chàh. Néih heui m̀h-heui a?
   我 哋 而 家 去 飲 茶 。 你 去 唔 去 呀 ？

10. Néih tái m̀h-tái dihn-sih a?
    你 睇 唔 睇 電 視 呀 ？

B. Like to : 'jùng-yi' 鍾意　*(Track 114)*

Affirmative statement

☞　jùng-yi + verb/noun　鍾意 ＋ 動詞／名詞

　　eg.　Ngóh jùng-yi yám chàh.
　　　　我 鍾 意 飲 茶 。
　　　　I like to drink tea.

　　　　Ngóh jùng-yi chàh.
　　　　我 鍾 意 茶 。
　　　　I like tea.

Negative statement

☞　m̀h-jùng-yi + verb/noun　唔 鍾意 ＋ 動詞／名詞

eg. Ngóh m̀h-jùng-yi yám chàh.

我 唔 鍾 意 飲 茶 。

I don't like to drink tea.

Ngóh m̀h-jùng-yi chàh.

我 唔 鍾 意 茶 。

I don't like tea.

Question form

☞ jùng m̀h-jùng-yi + verb/noun

鍾唔鍾意 + 動詞/名詞

eg. Néih jùng m̀h-jùng-yi yám chàh a?

你 鍾 唔 鍾 意 飲 茶 呀 ？

Do you like to drink tea?

Néih jùng m̀h-jùng-yi chàh a?

你 鍾 唔 鍾 意 茶 呀 ？

Do you like tea?

1. Néih jùng-yi jouh māt-yéh a?
   你 鍾 意 做 乜 嘢 呀 ？

2. Néih-deih jùng m̀h-jùng-yi tái dihn-sih ga?
   你 哋 鍾 唔 鍾 意 睇 電 視 㗎 ？

3. Ngóh jùng-yi sihk-yéh.
   我 鍾 意 食 嘢 。

4. Ngóh m̀h-jùng-yi máaih-yéh.
   我 唔 鍾 意 買 嘢 。

5. Ngóh hóu jùng-yi fan-gaau.
   我 好 鍾 意 瞓 覺 。

6. Ngóh jùng-yi daap syùhn.
   我 鍾 意 搭 船 。

7. Néih pàhng-yáuh jùng-yi māt-yéh dím-sām a?
   你 朋 友 鍾 意 乜 嘢 點 心 呀 ？

8. Ngóh m̀h-jùng-yi tái m̀h-hōi-sām ge hei.
   我 唔 鍾 意 睇 唔 開 心 嘅 戲 。

9. Léih táai jùng-yi māt-yéh sīk ga?
   李 太 鍾 意 乜 嘢 色 㗎 ？

10. Kéuih-deih m̀h-haih géi jùng-yi yám séui.
    佢 哋 唔 係 幾 鍾 意 飲 水 。

C. Want to : 'séung' 想 *(Track 115)*

Affirmative statement

☞ séung + verb 想 ＋ 動詞

　　eg. Ngóh séung yám séui.
　　　　我 想 飲 水 。
　　　　I want to drink water.

☞ séung yiu + noun 想要 ＋ 名詞

　　eg. Ngóh séung yiu yāt būi séui.
　　　　我 想 要 一 杯 水 。
　　　　I want a glass of water.

Negative statement

☞ m̀h-séung + verb 唔想 ＋ 動詞

　　eg. Ngóh m̀h-séung yám séui.
　　　　我 唔 想 飲 水 。
　　　　I don't want to drink water.

Question form

☞ séung m̀h-séung + verb + a? 想唔想 + 動詞 + 呀？

eg. Néih séung m̀h-séung yám séui a?

你 想 唔 想 飲 水 呀 ？

Do you want to drink water?

1. Kéuih m̀h-yiu chàh, kéuih séung yiu dung séui.
   佢 唔 要 茶 ， 佢 想 要 凍 水 。

2. Kéuih séung máaih nī-gihn sāam.
   佢 想 買 呢 件 衫 。

3. Kéuih séung tīng-yaht sahp-dím héi-sān.
   佢 想 聽 日 十 點 起 身 。

4. Ngóh yìh-gā séung heui sihk faahn.
   我 而 家 想 去 食 飯 。

5. Ngóh m̀h-séung fàan-gùng, ngóh séung fan-gaau.
   我 唔 想 返 工 ， 我 想 瞓 覺 。

6. Néih séung m̀h-séung tùhng kéuih sihk faahn a?
   你 想 唔 想 同 佢 食 飯 呀 ？

7. Ngóh séung tùhng pàhng-yáuh heui máaih-yéh.
   我 想 同 朋 友 去 買 嘢 。

8. Néih séung heui bīn-douh a?
   你 想 去 邊 度 呀 ？

9. Ngóh m̀h-séung hàahng-louh.
   我 唔 想 行 路 。

10. Néih sīng-kèih-yaht séung jouh māt-yéh a?
    你 星 期 日 想 做 乜 嘢 呀 ？

D. Hundred and Thousand *(Track 116)*

100	yāt baak	509	ńgh baak lìhng gáu
	一 百		五 百 零 九
101	yāt baak lìhng yāt	410	sei baak yāt sahp
	一 百 零 一		四 百 一 十
102	yāt baak lìhng yih	111	yāt baak yāt sahp yāt
	一 百 零 二		一 百 一 十 一
203	yih baak lìhng sàam	312	sàam baak yāt sahp yih
	二 百 零 三		三 百 一 十 二
604	luhk baak lìhng sei	913	gáu baak yāt sahp sàam
	六 百 零 四		九 百 一 十 三
905	gáu baak lìhng ńgh	514	ńgh baak yāt sahp sei
	九 百 零 五		五 百 一 十 四
306	sàam baak lìhng luhk	815	baat baak yāt sahp ńgh
	三 百 零 六		八 百 一 十 五
807	baat baak lìhng chāt	416	sei baak yāt sahp luhk
	八 百 零 七		四 百 一 十 六

*   *   *   *   *   *

729 chāt baak yih sahp gáu / chāt baak yah gáu
七 百 二 十 九 / 七 百 廿 九

238 yih baak sàam sahp baat / yih baak sà-ah baat
二 百 三 十 八 / 二 百 卅 八

1,000 yāt chìn
一 千

2,001 yih chìn lìhng yāt
二 千 零 一

3,010   sàam chìn lìhng yāt sahp
三 千 零 一 十

4,567   sei chìn ńgh baak luhk sahp chāt / sei chìn ńgh baak luhk-ah chāt
四 千 五 百 六 十 七

10,000 yāt maahn
一 萬

When numbers are followed by the next digit only

690   luhk baak gáu (sahp)
六 百 九 （十）

170   (yāt) baak chāt (sahp)
（一）百 七 （十）

250   yih baak ńgh (sahp) / léuhng baak ńgh (sahp)
二 百 五 （十）/ 兩 百 五 （十）

5,600   ńgh chìn luhk (baak)
五 千 六 （百）

8,900   baat chìn gáu (baak)
八 千 九 （百）

34,000 sàam maahn sei (chìn)
三 萬 四 （千）

PRACTICE

Read out the followings

1. 107	4. 70,002	7. 298.90	10. 132,567
2. $978	5. $615.70	8. $3,080	11. 801
3. 8,600	6. 4,321	9. 506	12. 2,700

PYRAMID DRILLS   *(Track 117)*

1.
dím-sām
點 心

sihk dím-sām
食 點 心

Néih sihk dím-sām
你 食 點 心

Néih m̀h-sihk dím-sām
你 唔 食 點 心

Néih sihk m̀h-sihk dím-sām a?
你 食 唔 食 點 心 呀 ？

2.
yám séui
飲 水

jùng-yi yám séui
鍾 意 飲 水

m̀h-jùng-yi yám séui
唔 鍾 意 飲 水

Kéuih m̀h-jùng-yi yám séui
佢 唔 鍾 意 飲 水

Kéuih jùng m̀h-jùng-yi yám séui a?
佢 鍾 唔 鍾 意 飲 水 呀 ？

3.
hàahng-louh
行 路

hàahng-louh heui
行 路 去

hàahng-louh heui Wāan-jái
行 路 去 灣 仔

séung hàahng-louh heui Wāan-jái

想　行　路　去　灣　仔

m̀h-séung hàahng-louh heui Wāan-jái

唔　想　行　路　去　灣　仔

Kéuih m̀h-séung hàahng-louh heui Wāan-jái

佢　唔　想　行　路　去　灣　仔

Kéuih séung m̀h-séung hàahng-louh heui Wāan-jái a?

佢　想　唔　想　行　路　去　灣　仔　呀　？

SUBSTITUTION DRILLS   *(Track 118)*

1. Ngóh jùng-yi <u>tái dihn-sih</u>. 我　鍾　意　<u>睇　電　視</u>　。

   a) yám chàh 飲茶

   b) daap bā-sí 搭巴士

   c) sihk chà-sìu faahn 食叉燒飯

   d) chēut heui 出去

2. Ngóh hóu séung <u>heui tái-hei</u>. 我　好　想　<u>去　睇　戲</u>　。

   a) faai-dī fàan ūk-kéi 快啲返屋企

   b) yám dung séui 飲凍水

   c) heui séuhng-tòhng 去上堂

   d) màaih-dāan 埋單

REVIEW EXERCISE

I.   Fill in the blanks

1. Ngóh jùng-yi _____ chàh.

   我　鍾　意　_____　茶　。

2. Chàhn síu-jé hóu báau. Kéuih _____ sihk-yéh la.

   陳　小　姐　好　飽　。　佢　_____　食　嘢　喇　。

3. Yám _____ séui a?

　飲 _____ 水 呀 ？

4. Néih séung yám _____ chàh a?

　你 想 飲 _____ 茶 呀 ？

5. Hòh sàang _____ hà-gáau a?

　何 生 _____ 蝦 餃 呀 ？

6. Ngóh séung máaih _____ .

　我 想 買 _____ 。

II. Rewrite the following sentences

1. pàhng-yáuh / sāam / máaih / kéuih / séung
　朋 友 / 衫 / 買 / 佢 / 想

2. yám / néih / m̀h / ga-fē / yám / a
　飲 / 你 / 唔 / 咖 啡 / 飲 / 呀

3. Chàhn / tái hei / jùng-yi / m̀h / sìn-sàang
　陳 / 睇 戲 / 鍾 意 / 唔 / 先 生

4. néih / sihk / bīn-go / faahn / tùhng / séung / a
　你 / 食 / 邊 個 / 飯 / 同 / 想 / 呀

5. séung / māt-yéh / néih / jouh / a / sīng-kèih-yaht
　想 / 乜 嘢 / 你 / 做 / 呀 / 星 期 日

III. Translation

1. What do you want?

2. Please give us four bowls of rice.

3. I don't like to go to movies with Mr Chan.

4. I want a glass of water.

5. She wants to buy a TV set.

6. Are you going to eat dim sum (drink tea) tomorrow?

7. Where do you want to go on Sunday?

8. What would you like to eat?

LISTENING EXERCISE

I. Listen to the dialogues and answer the questions   *(Track 119)*

1. _____   3. _____   5. _____

2. _____   4. _____

II. Listening comprehension   *(Track 120)*

1. _____   4. _____

2. _____   5. _____

3. _____   6. _____

Lesson 11

A Chinese dinner

A. At a Chinese restaurant   *(Track 121)*

Fùn-yìhng gwòng-làhm. Géi-dō wái a?
歡 迎 光 臨 。 幾 多 位 呀 ？
Welcome. How many persons?

Sei wái.
四 位 。
Four.

Chéng-mahn yáuh móuh dehng tói a?
請 問 有 冇 訂 枱 呀 ？
Have you made a reservation?

Yáuh.
有 。
Yes.

Gwai sing a?
貴 姓 呀 ？
May I know your name?

Sing Chàhn.

姓 陳 。

My name is Chan.

Chàhn sàang, m̀h-gòi nī-bihn lā.

陳 生 ， 唔 該 呢 邊 啦 。

Mr. Chan, this way please.

B.   Ordering   *(Track 122)*

Géi-wái yám dī māt-yéh a?

幾 位 飲 啲 乜 嘢 呀 ？

What would you like to drink?

Léuhng jì bē-jáu, yāt gwun hó-lohk, yāt būi gwán-séui.

兩 枝 啤 酒 ， 一 罐 可 樂 ， 一 杯 滾 水 。

Two bottles of beer, a can of coke, a glass of boiled water.

Séung sihk dī māt-yéh a?

想 食 啲 乜 嘢 呀 ？

What would you like to eat?

M̀h-gòi yāt gàn baahk-cheuk-hā, yāt tìuh jīng hùhng-bāan, yāt go sài-làahn-fā cháau daai-jí, juhng yiu yāt go yùh-hēung ké-jí tīm.

唔 該 一 斤 白 灼 蝦 、 一 條 蒸 紅 斑 、 一 個 西 蘭 花 炒 帶 子 ， 仲 要 一 個 魚 香 茄 子 添 。

A catty of steamed shrimp, a steamed red garoupa, sautéed scallop with broccoli, and braised egg plant with spicy garlic sauce please.

Yiu m̀h-yiu tòng a?

要 唔 要 湯 呀 ？

Do you want any soup?

Ṁh-sái la, m̀h-gòi.

唔 使 喇 ， 唔 該 。

No. Thanks.

(Then the dishes come.)

Yiu géi-dō go faahn a?

要 幾 多 個 飯 呀 ？

How many bowls of rice do you want?

Sei go faahn lā, m̀h-gòi.

四 個 飯 啦 ， 唔 該 。

Four bowls of rice please.

Ṁh-gòi béi léuhng deui gūng-faai ngóh-deih.

唔 該 畀 兩 對 公 筷 我 哋 。

Please give us two pairs of serving chopsticks.

> faai-ji 筷子：
> chopsticks (M: deui 對)
> gūng-faai 公筷：
> serving chopsticks

C. During dinner   *(Track 123)*

Sihk faahn. Yám būi!

食 飯 。 飲 杯 ！

Let's start to eat. Cheers!

Néih yiu m̀h-yiu dī choi a?

你 要 唔 要 啲 菜 呀 ？

Do you want some vegetables?

Ṁh-sái haak-hei. Jih-géi làih lā.

唔 使 客 氣 。 自 己 嚟 啦 。

Thank you. I'll help myself.

Nī tìuh yú hóu leng, si-háh lā.

呢 條 魚 好 靚 ， 試 吓 啦 。

The fish is good. Try it.

Ngóh gau la, m̀h-gòi. Néih sihk dō-dī lā.

我 夠 喇 ， 唔 該 。 你 食 多 啲 啦 。

Thanks, I had enough. You eat more.

Nī-dī hā hóu hóu-sihk.

呢 啲 蝦 好 好 食 。

The shrimp tastes good.

Haih a. Dī hā hóu leng.

係 呀 。 啲 蝦 好 靚 。

Yes, the shrimp is good.

Nī-wún faahn yāt yàhn yāt bun lā.

呢 碗 飯 一 人 一 半 啦 。

Let's share this bowl of rice.

Hóu aak. M̀h-gòi ngóh séung yám chàh.

好 呃 。 唔 該 我 想 飲 茶 。

OK. Excuse me, I want to drink some tea.

Móuh mahn-tàih, ngóh bōng néih lā.

冇 問 題 ， 我 幫 你 啦 。

No problem. Let me help you.

Móuh séui wo. M̀h-gòi gā séui.

冇 水 喎 。 唔 該 加 水 。

There's no water. Please refill the teapot.

Yiu m̀h-yiu tìhm-bán a?

要 唔 要 甜 品 呀 ？

Do you want any dessert?

M̀h-sái la, báau la.

唔 使 喇 ， 飽 喇 。

No, I'm full.

Ngóh-deih màaih-dāan lā.
我 哋 埋 單 啦 。
Let's get the bill.

Nī chāan ngóh chéng néih lā.
呢 餐 我 請 你 啦 。
This is my treat.

Dò-jeh.
多 謝 。
Thank you.

Drills for dining in a Chinese restaurant   *(Track 124)*

1. Yáuh māt-yéh bē-jáu a?
   有 乜 嘢 啤 酒 呀 ？
   What kind of beer do you have?

2. Yáuh māt-yéh dahk-ga a?
   有 乜 嘢 特 價 呀 ？
   Is there any special offer?

3. Dī lùhng-hā leng m̀h-leng a?
   啲 龍 蝦 靚 唔 靚 呀 ？
   Is the lobster good?

4. Tìuh yú yáuh géi-daaih a?
   條 魚 有 幾 大 呀 ？
   How big is the fish?

5. Yáuh móuh dōu cha a?
   有 冇 刀 叉 呀 ？
   Do you have knife and fork?

6. Yáuh móuh ngàh-chīm a?
   有 冇 牙 籤 呀 ？
   Do you have toothpicks?

7. Sàu m̀h-sàu kāat a?
   收 唔 收 卡 呀 ？
   Do you take credit card?

8. M̀h-gòi béi jèung dang ngóh.
   唔 該 畀 張 櫈 我 。
   Please give me a chair.

9. M̀h-gòi béi tìuh mòuh-gān ngóh.
   唔 該 畀 條 毛 巾 我 。
   Please give me a towel.

10. M̀h-gòi béi jek gāng ngóh.
    唔 該 畀 隻 羹 我 。
    Please give me a spoon.

Cantonese Dishes   (Track 125)

baahk cheuk hā 白灼蝦	Steamed shrimp
gwū lōu yuhk 咕嚕肉	Sweet and sour pork
sāi-làahn-fā cháau daai-jí 西蘭花炒帶子	Sautéed scallop w/ broccoli
syun yùhng sāi-làahn-fā 蒜蓉西蘭花	Sautéed broccoli w/ garlic
yùh hēung ké-jí 魚香茄子	Braised egg plant w/ spicy garlic sauce
sūk-máih bāan-faai 粟米班塊	Fried fish fillet in sweet corn sauce
jīu-yìhm sīn-yáu 椒鹽鮮魷	Deep fried squid w/ pepper salt
jīu-yìhm dauh-fuh 椒鹽豆腐	Deep fried bean curd w/ pepper salt

VOCABULARY *(Track 126)*

1. bē-jáu 啤酒   N : beer
   eg. yāt jì bē-jáu 一枝啤酒 : a bottle of beer
   yāt gwun bē-jáu 一罐啤酒 : a can of beer
   yāt būi sàang-bē 一杯生啤 : a glass of draft beer

2. yàhn 人   N : people
   eg. yāt go yàhn 一個人 : a person

3. syù 書   N : book
   eg. yāt bún syù 一本書 : a book
   tái syù 睇書 : read a book

4. dehng tói 訂枱   VO : reserve a table
   eg. yāt jèung tói 一張枱 : a table

5. yíng-séung 影相   VO : take a photo
   eg. yāt jèung séung 一張相 : a photo

6. dò 多   ADJ : many; much; plenty
   eg. hóu dò 好多 : plenty; a lot; many
   dò-dī 多啲 : some more

7. verb + jó 咗   VS : indicating an action completed

8. kàhm-máahn 琴晚   TW : last night

SENTENCE PATTERNS

A. Counting objects   *(Track 127)*

☞ number + measure + noun

數目 ＋ 量詞 ＋ 名詞

eg. yāt go yàhn

一　個　人

one person

☞ géi (-dō) + measure + noun + a?

幾（多） ＋ 量詞 ＋ 名詞 ＋ 呀？

eg. géi-dō go yàhn a?

幾 多 個 人 呀 ?

How many people?

1. Nī-douh yáuh yāt gihn sāam, haih bīn-go ga?
    呢 度 有 一 件 衫 ， 係 邊 個 㗎 ？

2. Kéuih sihk léuhng wún faahn.
    佢 食 兩 碗 飯 。

3. Ngóh yáuh sàam go pàhng-yáuh làih yám chàh.
    我 有 三 個 朋 友 嚟 飲 茶 。

4. Yāt ga dīk-sí chóh (*sit) géi-dō go yàhn a?
    一 架 的 士 坐 幾 多 個 人 呀 ？

5. Ngóh séung máaih yāt bún syù.
    我 想 買 一 本 書 。

6. M̀h-gòi bōng ngóh-deih yíng (yāt) jèung séung lā.
    唔 該 幫 我 哋 影 （一） 張 相 啦 。

7. Ṁh-gòi béi ńgh gwun bē-jáu ngóh.
唔　該　畀　五　罐　啤　酒　我　。

B.　Action in the recent past　*(Track 128)*

Affirmative statement

☞　verb + jó (+ la)　　詞　＋　咗　（＋喇）

eg. Ngóh sihk-jó faahn la.
我　食　咗　飯　喇　。
I have eaten already.

Negative statement

☞　móuh + verb 冇　＋　動詞

eg. Ngóh móuh sihk faahn.
我　冇　食　飯　。
I didn't eat.

Question form

☞　Yáuh móuh + verb + a?　有冇　＋　動詞　＋　呀？

eg. Kéuih yáuh móuh sihk faahn a?
佢　有　冇　食　飯　呀　？
Did he eat?

Answer: Yáuh. / Móuh.
有。/ 冇。
Yes. / No.

1. Chàhn sàang yáuh móuh sihk faahn a?
   陳 生 有 冇 食 飯 呀 ？

2. Ngóh móuh daap deih-tit làih.
   我 冇 搭 地 鐵 嚟 。

3. Néih kàhm-máahn yáuh móuh tái dihn-sih a?
   你 琴 晚 有 冇 睇 電 視 呀 ？

4. Kéuih-deih móuh dehng tói yám chàh.
   佢 哋 冇 訂 枱 飲 茶 。

5. Léih taai-táai yáuh móuh séuhng-tòhng a?
   李 太 太 有 冇 上 堂 呀 ？

6. Kéuih móuh làih yám chàh.
   佢 冇 嚟 飲 茶 。

7. Chàhn sìn-sàang yáuh móuh chēut heui a?
   陳 先 生 有 冇 出 去 呀 ？

8. Ngóh máaih-jó hóu dò syù.
   我 買 咗 好 多 書 。

9. Ngóh máaih-jó yāt bún Yīng-màhn (* English) syù.
   我 買 咗 一 本 英 文 書 。

10. Néih kàhm-yaht heui-jó bīn-douh a?
    你 琴 日 去 咗 邊 度 呀 ？

11. Kéuih tùhng bīn-go heui-jó máaih-yéh a?
    佢 同 邊 個 去 咗 買 嘢 呀 ？

12. Ngóh-deih luhk-dím-bun sihk-jó faahn la.
    我 哋 六 點 半 食 咗 飯 喇 。

13. Ngóh pàhng-yáuh làih-jó ngóh ūk-kéi.
    我 朋 友 嚟 咗 我 屋 企 。

14. Néih yíng-jó géi-dò jèung séung a?
    你 影 咗 幾 多 張 相 呀 ？

15. Néih tái-jó māt-yéh hei a?
    你 睇 咗 乜 嘢 戲 呀 ？

C. Need to : 'yiu' 要 and 'm̀h-sái' 唔使 *(Track 129)*

Affirmative statement

☞ yiu + verb/noun 要 + 動詞/名詞

eg. Ngóh yiu yám séui.
我 要 飲 水 。
I need to drink water.

Ngóh yiu séui.
我 要 水 。
I want water.

Negative statement

☞ m̀h-yiu + noun 唔要 + 名詞

eg. Ngóh m̀h-yiu séui.
我 唔 要 水 。
I don't want water.

☞ m̀h-sái + verb 唔使 + 動詞

eg. Ngóh m̀h-sái yám séui.
我 唔 使 飲 水 。
I don't need to drink water.

Question form

☞ yiu m̀h-yiu + noun + a? 要唔要 + 名詞 + 呀？

eg. Néih yiu m̀h-yiu séui a?
你 要 唔 要 水 呀 ？
Do you want any water?

Answer: Yiu. / M̀h-sái.

要 。 / 唔 使 。

Yes. / No.

☞ sái m̀h-sái + verb + a? 使唔使 + 動詞 + 呀 ?

eg. Néih sái m̀h-sái yám séui a?

你 使 唔 使 飲 水 呀 ?

Do you need to drink water?

Answer: Yiu. / M̀h-sái.

要 。 / 唔 使 。

Yes. / No.

1. Ngóh yiu hóu dò chín, ngóh séung máaih chē.
   我 要 好 多 錢 ， 我 想 買 車 。

2. Néih tīng-yaht sái m̀h-sái fàan-gùng a?
   你 聽 日 使 唔 使 返 工 呀 ？

3. Chàhn síu-jé yiu m̀h-yiu syù a?
   陳 小 姐 要 唔 要 書 呀 ？

4. Ngóh m̀h-sái sihk-yéh, ngóh m̀h-tóuh-ngoh.
   我 唔 使 食 嘢 ， 我 唔 肚 餓 。

5. Kéuih m̀h-yiu chàh, kéuih séung yiu dung séui.
   佢 唔 要 茶 ， 佢 想 要 凍 水 。

6. Ngóh chāt-dím-bun yiu fàan ūk-kéi.
   我 七 點 半 要 返 屋 企 。

7. Ngóh gàm-yaht yiu tùhng taai-táai heui máaih-yéh.
   我 今 日 要 同 太 太 去 買 嘢 。

8. Kéuih-deih wah m̀h-sái daap-chè, hàahng-louh heui dāk la.
   佢 哋 話 唔 使 搭 車 ， 行 路 去 得 喇 。

PYRAMID DRILLS   *(Track 130)*

1.
yāt jì bē-jáu
一　枝　啤　酒

yiu yāt jì bē-jáu
要　一　枝　啤　酒

séung yiu yāt jì bē-jáu
想　要　一　枝　啤　酒

Ngóh séung yiu yāt jì bē-jáu.
我　想　要　一　枝　啤　酒　。

2.
dehng tói
訂　枱

móuh dehng tói
冇　訂　枱

yáuh móuh dehng tói
有　冇　訂　枱

Léih sìn-sàang yáuh móuh dehng tói a?
李　先　生　有　冇　訂　枱　呀　？

3.
yíng-jó séung
影　咗　相

yíng-jó hóu dò séung
影　咗　好　多　相

Ngóh yíng-jó hóu dò séung.
我　影　咗　好　多　相　。

Ngóh tùhng pàhng-yáuh yíng-jó hóu dò séung.
我　同　朋　友　影　咗　好　多　相　。

4.

fàan-gùng
返 工

tīng-yaht fàan-gùng
聽 日 返 工

tīng-yaht m̀h-sái fàan-gùng
聽 日 唔 使 返 工

Néih tīng-yaht m̀h-sái fàan-gùng
你 聽 日 唔 使 返 工

Néih tīng-yaht sái m̀h-sái fàan-gùng a?
你 聽 日 使 唔 使 返 工 呀 ？

SUBSTITUTION DRILLS   *(Track 131)*

1. Néih gàm-yaht yáuh móuh <u>fàan-gùng</u> a?
   你 今 日 有 冇 <u>返 工</u> 呀 ？
   a) daap síu-bā 搭小巴   c) chēut heui 出去
   b) tái syù 睇書   d) yám chàh 飲茶

2. Kéuih béi-jó <u>yāt-bún syù</u> ngóh.
   佢 畀 咗 <u>一 本 書</u> 我 。
   a) yāt deui faai-jí 一對筷子   c) yāt jèung séung 一張相
   b) kéuih ge sàn dihn-wá   d) yih baak mān $200
      佢嘅新電話

3. Wòhng síu-jé yiu <u>yám bē-jáu</u>.
   黃 小 姐 要 <u>飲 啤 酒</u> 。
   a) máaih yéh 買嘢   c) ńgh-dím jáu 五點走
   b) fan-gaau 瞓覺   d) sihk faahn 食飯

4. Chàhn sìn-sàang m̀h-sái <u>sihk yéh</u>.

陳 先 生 唔 使 <u>食 嘢</u> 。

a) fàan ūk-kéi 返屋企   c) máaih syù 買書

b) daap bā-sí 搭巴士   d) dehng tói yám-chàh 訂枱飲茶

REVIEW EXERCISE

1.   Translation

1. I didn't give him a book.

2. I didn't go there.

3. My friend slept at 11:15 last night.

4. We took lots of photos.

5. His wife doesn't need to buy anything.

6. I drank two cups of tea.

7. Who did you give the receipt to?

8. We ate lots of dim sum. They were tasty.

9. I have to go home for dinner tomorrow.

10. We didn't take MTR to Central.

II.   Answer questions from a waiter when ordering   *(Track 132)*

1. Yiu m̀h-yiu tòng a?
   要 唔 要 湯 呀 ？
   Do you want some soup?

2. Jùng m̀h-jùng-yi sihk hói-sìn a?
   鍾 唔 鍾 意 食 海 鮮 呀 ？
   Do you like seafood?

3. Séung sihk māt-yéh yú a?
   想 食 乜 嘢 魚 呀 ？
   What kind of fish do you want?

4. Yiu m̀h-yiu tìhm-bán a?
   要 唔 要 甜 品 呀 ？
   Do you want any dessert?

5. Yiu géi-dò jek wún-jái a?
   要 幾 多 隻 碗 仔 呀 ？
   How many serving bowls do you want?

6. Yiu géi-dò jek būi a?
   要 幾 多 隻 杯 呀 ？
   How many cups/glasses do you want?

LISTENING EXERCISE   *(Track 133)*

Listen to the dialogues and choose the correct answer

1. _____   3. _____   5. _____   7. _____

2. _____   4. _____   6. _____   8. _____

Lesson 12

Where do you live?

CONVERSATION

A. Where do you work? *(Track 134)*

Néih hái bīn-douh fàan-gùng a?
你 喺 邊 度 返 工 呀 ？
Where do you work?

Ngóh hái Wāan-jái fàan-gùng.
我 喺 灣 仔 返 工 。
I work in Wan Chai.

Wāan-jái bīn-douh a?
灣 仔 邊 度 呀 ？
Where in Wan Chai?

Hái Jùng-wàahn Gwóng-chèuhng.
喺 中 環 廣 場 。
At Central Plaza.

Géi-dō láu a?
幾 多 樓 呀 ？
Which floor?

Sahp-baat láu.
十 八 樓 。
On the 18th floor.

B. Where do you live? *(Track 135)*

Hi! Hóu noih móuh gin. Néih yìh-gā hái bīn-douh jyuh a?
嗨 ！ 好 耐 冇 見 。 你 而 家 喺 邊 度 住 呀 ？
Hey! Haven't seen you for a long time. Where do you live now?

Ngóh hái Tùhng-lòh-wāan jyuh.
我 喺 銅 鑼 灣 住 。
I live in Causeway Bay.

Tùhng-lòh-wāan hóu fòng-bihn wo.
銅 鑼 灣 好 方 便 喎 。
Causeway Bay is a convenient place.

Haih a. Jàn-haih hóu fòng-bihn.
係 呀 。 真 係 好 方 便 。
Yes. It's really convenient.

Gám, néih hái bīn-douh fàan-gùng a?
咁 ， 你 喺 邊 度 返 工 呀 ？
Well, where do you work?

Ngóh hái Jùng-wàahn.
我 喺 中 環 。
I work in Central.

Ngóh dōu haih wo. Dāk-hàahn yāt-chàih sihk faahn lā.
我 都 係 喎 。 得 閒 一 齊 食 飯 啦 。
Me too. Let's have lunch together when you are free.

C.   Where shall we go for dinner?   *(Track 136)*

Ngóh-deih sīng-kèih-luhk heui bīn-douh sihk faahn a?

我 哋 星 期 六 去 邊 度 食 飯 呀 ？

Where shall we go for dinner on Saturday?

Heui Jìm-sà-jéui sihk Chìuh-jāu choi, hóu m̀h-hóu a?

去 尖 沙 咀 食 潮 洲 菜 ， 好 唔 好 呀 ？

Shall we go to Tsim Sha Tsui and have Chiuchow cuisine?

Gwóng-dūng Douh yáuh yāt gàan jáu-làuh hóu hóu-sihk ga.

廣 東 道 有 一 間 酒 樓 好 好 食 㗎 。

There is a good restaurant on Canton Road.

Hóu, gàan jáu-làuh hái bīn-douh a?

好 ， 間 酒 樓 喺 邊 度 呀 ？

Good, where is the restaurant?

Hái Gwóng-dùng Douh baat-sahp-baat houh.

喺 廣 東 道 八 十 八 號 。

It is on 88 Canton Road.

Hái géi-dō láu a?

喺 幾 多 樓 呀 ？

On which floor?

Hái deih-há ge.

喺 地 下 嘅 。

It is on ground floor.

Géi-dō dím a?

幾 多 點 呀 ？

What time?

Chāt-dím-bun hóu m̀h-hóu a?

七 點 半 好 唔 好 ？

What about 7:30?

Hóu, néih dehng tói lā.
好 ， 你 訂 枱 啦 。
Good, please make the reservation.

READING   *(Track 137)*

Ngóh haih Chàhn Ji-Mìhng, jyuh hái Tùhng-lòh-wāan, gūng-sī hái Gām-jūng.
我 係 陳 志 明 ， 住 喺 銅 鑼 灣 ， 公 司 喺 金 鐘 。
I am Chan Chi Ming. I live in Causeway Bay. My office is in Admiralty.

Ngóh yaht-yaht daap dīk-sí fàan-gùng. Hèung-góng ge dīk-sí hóu pèhng, hóu
我 日 日 搭 的 士 返 工 。 香 港 嘅 的 士 好 平 ， 好
Everyday I go to work by taxi. Taxis in Hong Kong are cheap and

fòng-bihn. Ngóh yāt-dím sihk faahn, jeui jùng-yi tùhng tùhng-sih heui yám chàh.
方 便 。 我 一 點 食 飯 ， 最 鍾 意 同 同 事 去 飲 茶 。
convenient. I have lunch at 1:00. I like to go for tea with my colleagues the best.

Ngóh-deih sìh-sìh hái Méih-Sām Jáu-làuh yám-chàh. Méih-Sām ge dím-sām
我 哋 時 時 喺 美 心 酒 樓 飲 茶 。 美 心 嘅 點 心
We often go to Maxim's Restaurant to have tea.   The dim sum at Maxim's are

hóu hóu-sihk. Ngóh luhk-dím sàu-gùng. Yeh-máahn ngóh hái ūk-kéi sihk faahn.
好 好 食 。 我 六 點 收 工 。 夜 晚 我 喺 屋 企 食 飯 。
very delicious. I finish work at 6:00. In the evening, I eat at home.

VOCABULARY　*(Track 138)*

1. Gām-jūng 金鐘　　　　　　　PW : Admiralty
2. Tùhng-lòh-wāan 銅鑼灣　　　PW : Causeway Bay
3. Jìm-sà-jéui 尖沙咀　　　　　PW : Tsim Sha Tsui
4. jyuh 住　　　　　　　　　　　V : live
5. sàu-gùng 收工　　　　　　　VO : finish work; leave office
6. mùhn-háu 門口 (M: go 個)　　N : entrance; doorway
7. gūng-sī 公司　　　　　　　　N : company; office
8. jáu-làuh 酒樓 (M: gàan 間)　N : Chinese restaurant
   eg. yāt gāan jáu-làuh 一間酒樓 : a Chinese restaurant

9. láu 樓　　　　　　　　　　　N : floor
   eg. gáu láu 九樓 : 9th floor
   　　deih-há 地下 : ground floor
   　　géi-dō láu 幾多樓 : which floor?

10. hái 喺　　　　　　　　　　　P : located at, in or on
11. yaht yaht 日日　　　　　　　PH : everyday
12. yeh-máahn 夜晚　　　　　　TW : in the evening
13. gàm-máahn 今晚　　　　　　TW : tonight
14. fòng-bihn 方便　　　　　　　ADJ : convenient
15. jàn-haih 真係　　　　　　　ADV : really
16. wo 喎　　　　　　　　　　　FP : implies telling new situation;
   　　　　　　　　　　　　　　　　 to remind

SENTENCE PATTERNS

A. Subject + place + verb *(Track 139)*

Affirmative statement

☞ Subject + hái + place + verb

主詞 ＋ 喺 ＋ 地方 ＋ 動詞

eg. Ngóh hái Wāan-jái fàan-gùng.

我 喺 灣 仔 返 工 。

I work in Wan Chai.

Negative statement

☞ Subject + m̀h-hái + place + verb

主詞 ＋ 唔喺 ＋ 地方 ＋ 動詞

eg. Ngóh m̀h-hái Wāan-jái fàan-gùng.

我 唔 喺 灣 仔 返 工 。

I don't work in Wan Chai.

Question form

☞ Subject + hái bīn-douh + verb + a?

主詞 ＋ 喺邊度 ＋ 動詞 ＋ 呀？

eg. Néih hái bīn-douh fàan-gùng a?

你 喺 邊 度 返 工 呀 ？

Where do you work?

1. Ngóh-deih ge gūng-sī hái Wāan-jái.
   我 哋 嘅 公 司 喺 灣 仔 。

2. Hòh síu-jé hái Tùhng-lòh-wāan máaih-yéh.
   何 小 姐 喺 銅 鑼 灣 買 嘢 。

3. Ngóh hái Jùng-wàahn tái-hei.
   我 喺 中 環 睇 戲 。

4. Dihn-wá hái gó-douh.
   電 話 喺 嗰 度 。

5. Kéuih jùng-yi hái Jìm-sà-jéui yám-chàh.
   佢 鍾 意 喺 尖 沙 咀 飲 茶 。

6. Néih-deih hái bīn-douh sihk faahn a?
   你 哋 喺 邊 度 食 飯 呀 ？

7. Ngóh jyuh hái yah-yih láu.
   我 住 喺 廿 二 樓 。

8. Kéuih hái bīn-douh jyuh a?
   佢 喺 邊 度 住 呀 ？

9. Ngóh hái mùhn-háu dáng néih.
   我 喺 門 口 等 你 。

10. Néih hái bīn-douh daap-chè fàan ūk-kéi a?
    你 喺 邊 度 搭 車 返 屋 企 呀 ？

B. People + time + place + action *(Track 140)*

☞ Subject + time + place + verb
主詞 + 時間 + 地方 + 動詞

eg. Ngóh yāt-dím hái Jùng-wàahn sihk faahn.
我 一 點 喺 中 環 食 飯 。
I have lunch in Central at 1:00.

1. Ngóh kàhm-máahn hái ūk-kéi tái dihn-sih.
   我 琴 晚 喺 屋 企 睇 電 視 。

2. Néih-deih sīng-kèih-luhk hái bīn-douh yíng-séung a?
   你 哋 星 期 六 喺 邊 度 影 相 呀 ？

3. Néih gàm-máahn hái bīn-douh tái-hei a?
   你 今 晚 喺 邊 度 睇 戲 呀 ？

4. Néih yìh-gā hái bīn-douh séuhng-tòhng a?
   你 而 家 喺 邊 度 上 堂 呀 ？

5. Ngóh-deih ńgh-dím-sei hái Sùhng-gwòng (*Sogo Department Store)
   mùhn-háu dáng.
   我 哋 五 點 四 喺 崇 光 門 口 等 。

6. Sīng-kèih-yaht hái bīn-douh yám-chàh a?
   星 期 日 喺 邊 度 飲 茶 呀 ？

7. Néih géi dím hái gūng-sī jáu a?
   你 幾 點 喺 公 司 走 呀 ？

8. Kéuih-deih tīng-yaht chāt-dím-bun hái jáu-làuh sihk faahn.
   佢 哋 聽 日 七 點 半 喺 酒 樓 食 飯 。

C. Giving suggestion   *(Track 141)*

☞ Suggestion + hóu m̀h-hóu a?
   建 議 ＋ 好 唔 好 呀 ？   Is it fine?/Is that alright?

   eg. Sàam-dím, hóu m̀h-hóu a?
   三 點 ， 好 唔 好 呀 ？
   How about 3:00?

   Answer: Hóu. / M̀h-hóu.
   好 。 / 唔好 。
   Fine. / No.

1. Ngóh-deih heui yám chàh, hóu m̀h-hóu a?
   我 哋 去 飲 茶 ， 好 唔 好 呀 ？

2. Faai-dī sàu-gùng hóu m̀h-hóu a?
   快 啲 收 工 好 唔 好 呀 ？

3. Gàm-yaht yāt-chàih sihk faahn, hóu m̀h-hóu a?
   今 日 一 齊 食 飯 ， 好 唔 好 呀 ？

4. Ngóh-deih hái mùhn-háu dáng, hóu m̀h-hóu a?
   我 哋 喺 門 口 等 ， 好 唔 好 呀 ？

5. Yám hó-lohk, hóu m̀h-hóu a?
   飲 可 樂 ， 好 唔 好 呀 ？

6. Ngóh-deih yāt-chàih heui máaih-yéh, hóu m̀h-hóu a?
   我 哋 一 齊 去 買 嘢 ， 好 唔 好 呀 ？

7. Heui gó-douh yíng-séung, hóu m̀h-hóu a?
   去 嗰 度 影 相 ， 好 唔 好 呀 ？

8. Máaih nī-go sàn ge, hóu m̀h-hóu a?
   買 呢 個 新 嘅 ， 好 唔 好 呀 ？

PYRAMID DRILLS *(Track 142)*

1.
                    Tùhng-lòh-wāan
                       銅 鑼 灣

                 hái Tùhng-lòh-wāan
                   喺 銅 鑼 灣

               hái Tùhng-lòh-wāan jyuh
                 喺 銅 鑼 灣 住

             Kéuih hái Tùhng-lòh-wāan jyuh
               佢 喺 銅 鑼 灣 住

           Kéuih m̀h-hái Tùhng-lòh-wāan jyuh.
             佢 唔 喺 銅 鑼 灣 住 。

2.
                    Wāan-jái
                     灣 仔

                  hái Wāan-jái
                   喺 灣 仔

hái Wāan-jái máaih-yéh
喺 灣 仔 買 嘢

kàhm-yaht hái Wāan-jái máaih-yéh
琴 日 喺 灣 仔 買 嘢

Néih kàhm-yaht hái Wāan-jái máaih-yéh
你 琴 日 喺 灣 仔 買 嘢

Néih kàhm-yaht tùhng pàhng-yáuh hái Wāan-jái máaih-yéh.
你 琴 日 同 朋 友 喺 灣 仔 買 嘢 。

SUBSTITUTION DRILLS   *(Track 143)*

1. Ngóh hái <u>Jùng-wàahn</u> jyuh. 我 喺 中 環 住 。

   a) Jìm-sà-jéui 尖沙咀   c) deih-há 地下

   b) luhk láu 六樓   d) Tùhng-lòh-wāan 銅鑼灣

2. Kéuih gàm-máahn hái Jìm-sà-jéui <u>máaih-yéh</u>.
   佢 今 晚 喺 尖 沙 咀 買 嘢 。

   a) yám jáu 飲酒   c) sihk faahn 食飯

   b) tái-hei 睇戲   d) jyuh 住

REVIEW EXERCISE

I. Rewrite the following sentences

1. ngóh / sahp baat / hái / láu / gūng-sī / ge
   我 / 十 八 / 喺 / 樓 / 公 司 / 嘅

2. bīn-douh / a / néih / hái / jyuh
   邊 度 / 呀 / 你 / 喺 / 住

3. gūng-sī / Jùng-wàahn / nī-gàan / hái / m̀h
   公 司 / 中 環 / 呢 間 / 喺 / 唔

4. bīn-go / a / fáan-gùng / hái / Wāan-jái
   邊 個 / 呀 / 返 工 / 喺 / 灣 仔

5. ge / Jìm-sà-jéui / pàhng-yáuh / jyuh / ngóh / hái
   嘅 / 尖 沙 咀 / 朋 友 / 住 / 我 / 喺

6. chàh / Léih sìn-sàang / láu / sàam / hái / yám
   茶 / 李 先 生 / 樓 / 三 / 喺 / 飲

7. jyuh / ngóh / hái / Tùhng-lòh-wāan / m̀h
   住 / 我 / 喺 / 銅 鑼 灣 / 唔

II. Translation

1. Do you like this Chinese restaurant?
2. I live in Tsim Sha Tsui.
3. Where does your friend work?
4. I eat at home today.
5. Where were you at 2:30?
6. My office is on the 25th floor.
7. I have dinner with my friends in Wan Chai.
8. Where was Mr Chan yesterday?
9. I was not shopping in Causeway Bay.
10. Where is the restaurant?
11. What time shall we meet at the entrance?
12. Tonight is really hot.

III. Study the plan of this department store, answer the questions.
(Track 144)

6/F	Stationery (màhn-geuih) 文具 Books (syù) 書 Cameras (séung-gēi) 相機
5/F	Electrical appliances (dihn-hei) 電器 Kitchen ware (chyùh-geuih) 廚具
4/F	Toys (wuhn-geuih) 玩具 Furniture (gà-sì) 傢俬
3/F	Sportswear (tái-yuhk yuhng-bán) 體育用品 Men's wear (nàahm jōng) 男裝
2/F	Ladies' wear (néuih jōng) 女裝 Shoes (hàaih) 鞋 Bags (dói) 袋
G/F	Cosmetics (fa-jōng-bán) 化妝品 Accessories (sáu-sīk) 首飾
B1	Supermarket (chìu-kāp síh-chèuhng) 超級市場

1. Sàam láu haih m̀h-haih chìu-kāp síh-chèuhng a?
   三 樓 係 唔 係 超 級 市 場 呀 ？

2. Ngóh taai-táai yiu máaih hàaih, heui géi-dō láu a?
   我 太 太 要 買 鞋 ， 去 幾 多 樓 呀 ？

3. Fa-jōng-bán haih m̀h-haih hái deih-há a?
   化 妝 品 係 唔 係 喺 地 下 呀 ？

4. Ngóh séung máaih wuhn-geuih, heui sei láu ngāam m̀h-ngāam (*correct) a?
   我 想 買 玩 具 ， 去 四 樓 啱 唔 啱 呀 ？

5. Ngóh hóu tóuh-ngoh, séung máaih yéh sihk, ngóh heui géi-dō láu a?
   我 好 肚 餓 ， 想 買 嘢 食 ， 我 去 幾 多 樓 呀 ？

6. Tùhng jōng (*Children's wear) hái géi-dō láu a?
   童 裝 喺 幾 多 樓 呀 ？

7. Ńgh láu yáuh móuh wún maaih (*sell) a?
   五 樓 有 冇 碗 賣 呀 ？

8. Ngóh séung máaih yāt go dói, heui yih láu ngāam m̀h-ngāam a?
   我 想 買 一 個 袋 ， 去 二 樓 啱 唔 啱 呀 ？

9. Máaih bāt (*pen) máaih syù, heui géi-dō láu a?
   買 筆 買 書 ， 去 幾 多 樓 呀 ？

10. Hái géi-dō láu yáuh dihn-sih-gēi (*TV set) maaih a?
    喺 幾 多 樓 有 電 視 機 賣 呀 ？

IV. Make conversations to invite your friends

Example:

Ngóh-deih heui <u>yám chàh</u>, hóu m̀h-hóu a?
我 哋 去 <u>飲 茶</u> ， 好 唔 好 呀 ？

Hóu a. Géi-dō dím heui a?
好 呀 。 幾 多 點 去 呀 ？

<u>Sahp-yih-dím-bun</u> hóu m̀h-hóu a?
<u>十 二 點 半</u> 好 唔 好 呀 ？

Hóu. Ngóh-deih hái <u>Sùhng-gwòng</u> (*Sogo Department Store) dáng lā.
好 。 我 哋 喺 崇 光 等 啦 。

Hóu lā. Yāt-jahn gin. (*See you later)
好 啦 。 一 陣 見 。

Substituton

a) máaih-yéh 買嘢
   2:45
   Tīn-sīng Máh-Tàuh 天星碼頭：Star Ferry

b) yám yéh 飲嘢
   5:30
   Ji-deih Gwóng-chèuhng
   置地廣場：The Landmark

c) sihk-fahhn 食飯
   1:00
   Deih-tit-jaahm Hàhng-sāng Ngàhn-hòhng
   地鐵站恒生銀行：Hang Seng Bank at MTR station

d) yám chàh 飲茶
   9:30
   Méih-sām Jáu-làuh 美心酒樓：Maxim's Restaurant

V.   Review on asking questions

A.   géi (dō) 幾(多)：asking a number

1. How much is it?

2. What time is it?

3. What number is this bus?

4. Which month?

5. What date is it today?

6. What is the discount?

7. How many people are there?

8. How many bowls of rice?

9. How many friends are coming?

10. How many cups of coffee?

11. How many cans of beer?

12. How many books?

13. When is your birthday? (*sāang-yaht 生日)

14. What day did you go for dim sum?

15. What is your phone number?

B.   māt-yéh 乜嘢 : asking the name

1. What color is this?

2. What transportation do you take?

3. What do you want?

4. What do you do on Saturday?

5. What do you like to eat?

6. Which tea do you drink?

C.   bīn 邊 : asking which one

1. Where is it?

2. Which cup is tea, which cup is coffee?

3. Which of these clothes are yours?

4. Who are you?

5. Which colleague?

6. Which day are you free?

D   dihng 定 : or?

1. Stay here or take away?

2. Hot or cold?

3. Bigger or smaller?

4. Red or blue?

5. Today or tomorrow?

6. You or me?

7. USA or China?

8. Central or Causeway Bay?

LISTENING EXERCISE

I.   Listen to the dialogues and answer the questions   *(Track 145)*

1. _____   5. _____

2. _____   6. _____

3. _____   7. _____

4. _____   8. _____

II.   Choose the appropriate Cantonese translation   *(Track 146)*

1. He doesn't live in Causeway Bay.   _____

2. My office is on the 24th floor.   _____

3. I like this Chinese restaurant.   _____

Lesson 13

Weather and date

A. It may rain tomorrow *(Track 147)*

 Tīng-yaht fong-ga, ngóh-deih heui léuih-hàhng, hóu m̀h-hóu a?
聽 日 放 假 ， 我 哋 去 旅 行 ， 好 唔 好 呀 ？
Tomorrow is a holiday, shall we go on an outing?

 Daahn-haih tīng-yaht tìn-hei màh-má-déi, waahk-jé lohk-yúh.
但 係 聽 日 天 氣 麻 麻 哋 ， 或 者 落 雨 。
However, the weather tomorrow is not very good, maybe it will rain.

 Gám, ngóh-deih hah-go láih-baai heui, hóu m̀h-hóu a?
咁 ， 我 哋 下 個 禮 拜 去 ， 好 唔 好 呀 ？
Well, shall we go next week?

 Hóu a. Hēi-mohng hah-go láih-baai ge tìn-hei wúih hóu-dī lā.
好 呀 。 希 望 下 個 禮 拜 嘅 天 氣 會 好 啲 啦 。
OK. I hope the weather next week will be better.

B.   There will be a meeting on the 18th of June   *(Track 148)*

Luhk-yuht sahp-baat-houh hòi-wúi, néih jì m̀h-jì a?
六 月 十 八 號 開 會 ， 你 知 唔 知 呀 ？
Do you know there is a meeting on 18th June.

Sahp-baat houh haih sīng-kèih-géi a?
十 八 號 係 星 期 幾 呀 ？
What day is the 18th?

Haih hah-go sīng-kèih-yih.
係 下 個 星 期 二 。
That is next Tuesday.

Géi-dím hòi-wúi a?
幾 點 開 會 呀 ？
What time is the meeting?

Aan-jau sàam-dím. Gei-dāk làih a!
晏 晝 三 點 。 記 得 嚟 呀 ！
It is 3 o'clock in the afternoon. Please remember to come.

Dāk la. Haih lak, nī-go wúi hòi dou géi-dím ga?
得 喇 。 係 嘞 ， 呢 個 會 開 到 幾 點 㗎 ？
OK. By the way, what time will this meeting end?

Nī-go wúi hòi dou luhk-dím.
呢 個 會 開 到 六 點 。
This meeting lasts until 6:00.

READING   *(Track 149)*

Hēung-góng   ge   tìn-hei,   m̀h-haih   géi   syù-fuhk.   Hái   Hèung-góng,
香 港 嘅 天 氣 唔 係 幾 舒 服 。 喺 香 港 ，
The weather in Hong Kong is not very comfortable. In Hong Kong,

yih-yuht yáuh-sìh hóu dung. Sàam-yuht, sei-yuht hóu sāp, sìh-sìh
二　月　有　時　好　凍　。　三　月　、　四　月　好　濕　，　時　時
sometimes is very cold in February. In March and April, it is very wet and often

yàm-tìn. Ngh-luhk-yuht sìh-sìh lohk daaih yúh. Luhk-yuht dou gáu-yuht
陰　天　。　五　、　六　月　時　時　落　大　雨　。　六　月　到　九　月
cloudy. It often rains hard in May and June. From June to September,

yiht dou sàam-sahp géi douh, juhng wúih dá-fùng. Sahp-yuht
熱　到　三　十　幾　度　，　仲　會　打　風　。　十　月
the temperature goes high up to over 30°C, and there will be typhoon. In October,

hòi-chí m̀h-haih géi yiht. Jeui hóu-tìn haih sahp-yāt-yuht dou yāt-yuht,
開　始　唔　係　幾　熱　。　最　好　天　係　十　一　月　到　一　月　，
it becomes not so hot. The best weather is from November to January,

hóu síu lohk yúh, yih sahp douh dóu, jàn-haih hóu syù-fuhk.
好　少　落　雨　，　二　十　度　倒　，　真　係　好　舒　服　。
it seldom rains, the temperature is around 20°C, it is really comfortable.

VOCABULARY   *(Track 150)*

1. tìn-hei 天氣	N :	weather
2. hóu-tìn 好天	ADJ :	fine weather
3. lohk yúh 落雨	VO :	rain
4. yàm-tìn 陰天	N :	cloudy
5. géi-sìh 幾時	QW :	when
6. seuhng-go yuht 上個月	TW :	last month
7. nī-go yuht 呢個月 / gàm go yuht 今個月	TW :	this month
8. hah-go yuht 下個月	TW :	next month

9. seuhng-go sīng-kèih 上個星期 /　　　TW : last week
   seuhng-go láih-baai 上個禮拜
   eg. seuhng-go sīng-kèih-luhk 上個星期六 : last Saturday

10. nī-go sīng-kèih 呢個星期 /　　　　TW : this week
    gàm-go sīng-kèih 今個星期 /
    nī-go láih-baai 呢個禮拜 /
    gàm-go láih-baai 今個禮拜

11. hah-go sīng-kèih 下個星期 /　　　　TW : next week
    hah-go láih-baai 下個禮拜

12. jì 知　　　　　　　　　　　　　　V : to know a fact

13. gei-dāk 記得　　　　　　　　　　V : remember
    eg. m̀h-gei-dāk 唔記得 : forget

14. léuih-hàhng 旅行　　　　　　　　N : travel; trip; picnic;
    　　　　　　　　　　　　　　　　　　outing

15. fong-ga 放假　　　　　　　　　　VO : on holiday; on vacation;
    　　　　　　　　　　　　　　　　　　on leave

16. hòi-wúi 開會　　　　　　　　　　VO : to hold a meeting
    eg. yāt go wúi 一個會: a meeting

17. hòi-chí 開始　　　　　　　　　　V : begin

18. syù-fuhk 舒服　　　　　　　　　ADJ : comfortable
    eg. m̀h-syù-fuhk 唔舒服 : uncomfortable; sick

19. daahn-haih 但係　　　　　　　　CON : but; however

20. jeui 最　　　　　　　　　　　　P : most

21. dou 到　　　　　　　　　　　　CON : until; to
    　　　　　　　　　　　　　　　　V : arrive

22. sìh-sìh 時時　　　　　　　　　　ADV : very often, always

23. yáuh-sìh 有時　　　　　　　　　ADV : sometimes

24. hóu-síu 好少　　　　　　　　　　ADV : seldom; rarely

SENTENCE PATTERNS

A. Drill on sentences with dates   *(Track 151)*

1. Sīng-kèih-luhk-yaht dōu yiu séuhng-tòhng.
   星 期 六 、 日 都 要 上 堂 。

2. Kéuih seuhng-go-yuht heui-jó léuih-hàhng.
   佢 上 個 月 去 咗 旅 行 。

3. Ngóh-deih ńgh-yuht sahp-chāt-houh sàam-dím hòi-wúi.
   我 哋 五 月 十 七 號 三 點 開 會 。

4. Gáu-yuht yah-sàam-houh fong-ga. Jì m̀h-jì fong māt-yéh ga a?
   九 月 廿 三 號 放 假 。 知 唔 知 放 乜 嘢 假 呀 ?

5. Hah-go-yuht sahp ńgh houh dī tùhng-sih yāt-chàih heui sihk faahn.
   下 個 月 十 五 號 啲 同 事 一 齊 去 食 飯 。

6. Hah-go sīng-kèih-luhk haih sei-yuht sahp-luhk-houh.
   下 個 星 期 六 係 四 月 十 六 號 。

7. Sahp-yuht yāt-houh m̀h-sái fàan-gùng, ngóh-deih heui bīn-douh wáan a?
   十 月 一 號 唔 使 返 工 ， 我 哋 去 邊 度 玩 呀 ?

8. Chāt-yuht yah-yih-houh, sīng-kèih-sàam daaih-hah (*a building) móuh séui, gei-dāk la.
   七 月 廿 二 號 、 星 期 三 大 廈 冇 水 ， 記 得 喇 。

9. Néih géi-sìh làih nī-gàan gūng-sī ga?
   你 幾 時 嚟 呢 間 公 司 㗎 ?

10. Kéuih pàhng-yáuh géi-sìh heui léuih-hàhng a?
    佢 朋 友 幾 時 去 旅 行 呀 ?

11. Néih géi-sìh heui Jìm-sà-jéui máaih-yéh a?
    你 幾 時 去 尖 沙 咀 買 嘢 呀 ?

12. Néih géi-sìh dāk-hàahn yāt-chàih sihk faahn a?
    你 幾 時 得 閒 一 齊 食 飯 呀 ?

B.   How often   *(Track 152)*

☞   Subject + adverb of frequency + time + place + verb
主語 ＋ 副詞 ＋ 時間詞 ＋ 地方 ＋ 動詞

1. Ngóh sìh-sìh tùhng tùhng-sih heui yám-chàh.
   我 時 時 同 同 事 去 飲 茶 。

2. Ngóh yáuh-sìh chāt-dím-bun sihk faahn, yáuh-sìh baat-dím sihk.
   我 有 時 七 點 半 食 飯 ， 有 時 八 點 食 。

3. Kéuih hóu-síu heui léuih-hàhng.
   佢 好 少 去 旅 行 。

4. Néih haih m̀h-haih sìh-sìh sahp-yāt-dím fan-gaau ga?
   你 係 唔 係 時 時 十 一 點 瞓 覺 㗎 ？

5. Ngóh yáuh-sìh hái gūng-sī sihk faahn, yàn-waih m̀h-séung chēut heui sihk.
   我 有 時 喺 公 司 食 飯 ， 因 為 唔 想 出 去 食 。

6. Ngóh hóu-síu tái dihn-sih, yàn-waih móuh yéh hóu tái.
   我 好 少 睇 電 視 ， 因 為 冇 嘢 好 睇 。

7. Kéuih yáuh-sìh daap síu-bā, yáuh-sìh daap dīk-sí fàan-gùng.
   佢 有 時 搭 小 巴 ， 有 時 搭 的 士 返 工 。

8. Ngóh-deih hóu-síu daap bā-sī fàan ūk-kéi, yàn-waih hóu màh-fàahn.
   我 哋 好 少 搭 巴 士 返 屋 企 ， 因 為 好 麻 煩 。

9. Ngóh sìh-sìh m̀h-dāk-hàahn séuhng-tòhng.
   我 時 時 唔 得 閒 上 堂 。

10. Kéuih-deih heui léuih-hàhng hóu-síu yíng-séung.
    佢 哋 去 旅 行 好 少 影 相 。

PRACTICE

Answer the following questions in Cantonese

1. How often do you see a movie in Central?

2. How often do you go shopping in Mong Kok (*Wohng-gok 旺角)?

3. How often do you watch TV?

4. How often do you have a meeting?

5. How often do you travel?

6. How often do you take a taxi to work?

7. Do you often miss your class?

8. Does it rain frequently in August?

C. Until, to : 'dou' 到   *(Track 153)*

1. Hah-go yuht sahp houh dou sahp-luhk houh fong-ga.
   下 個 月 十 號 到 十 六 號 放 假 。

2. Láih-baai-yāt dou láih-baai-sàam, ngóh dōu m̀h-dāk-hàahn.
   禮 拜 一 到 禮 拜 三 ， 我 都 唔 得 閒 。

3. Sahp-yih-dím-bun dou léuhng-dím sihk faahn.
   十 二 點 半 到 兩 點 食 飯 。

4. Ngóh gàm-go-yuht ńgh-houh dou baat-houh heui léuih-hàhng.
   我 今 個 月 五 號 到 八 號 去 旅 行 。

5. Tīng-yaht hòi-wúi hòi dou sàam-dím.
   聽 日 開 會 開 到 三 點 。

6. Jùng-wàahn heui dou Jìm-sà-jéui, daap syùhn jeui syù-fuhk.
   中 環 去 到 尖 沙 咀 ， 搭 船 最 舒 服 。

PRACTICE

Answer the following questions in Cantonese

1. What are your working hours?

2. What are the opening hours of shops?

3. What days does the bank open?

4. If I go from Causeway Bay to Wan Chai, which transport should I take?

D. But : 'daahn-haih' 但係 *(Track 154)*

1. Ngóh hóu jùng-yi yíng-séung, daahn-haih ngóh taai-táai m̀h-jùng-yi.
   我 好 鍾 意 影 相 ， 但 係 我 太 太 唔 鍾 意 。

2. Kàhm-yaht hóu hóu-tìn, daahn-haih gàm-yaht lohk-yúh.
   琴 日 好 好 天 ， 但 係 今 日 落 雨 。

3. Ngóh kàhm-máahn móuh fan-gaau, daahn-haih yih-gā m̀h-gwuih.
   我 琴 晚 冇 瞓 覺 ， 但 係 而 家 唔 劫 。

4. Ngóh séung séuhng-tòhng, daahn-haih yiu hòi-wúi.
   我 想 上 堂 ， 但 係 要 開 會 。

5. Chāt-yuht hóu yiht, daahn-haih yāt-yuht hóu dung.
   七 月 好 熱 ， 但 係 一 月 好 凍 。

6. Chàhn síu-jé móuh sihk faahn, daahn-haih kéuih m̀h-tóuh-ngoh.
   陳 小 姐 冇 食 飯 ， 但 係 佢 唔 肚 餓 。

PYRAMID DRILLS *(Track 155)*

1.   léuih-hàhng
   旅 行

   heui léuih-hàhng
   去 旅 行

   Ngóh heui léuih-hàhng
   我 去 旅 行

Ngóh láih-baai-ńgh heui léuih-hàhng
我　禮　拜　五　去　旅　行

Ngóh láih-baai-sàam dou láih-baai-ńgh heui léuih-hàhng.
我　禮　拜　三　到　禮　拜　五　去　旅　行　。

2.
lohk yúh
落　雨

kàhm-yaht lohk yúh
琴　日　落　雨

Gàm-yaht hóu hóu-tìn, kàhm-yaht lohk yúh
今　日　好　好　天　，　琴　日　落　雨

Gàm-yaht hóu hóu-tìn, daahn-haih kàhm-yaht lohk yúh.
今　日　好　好　天　，　但　係　琴　日　落　雨　。

3.
heui Jìm-sà-jéui
去　尖　沙　咀

daap-syùhn heui Jìm-sà-jéui
搭　船　去　尖　沙　咀

Néih daap-syùhn heui Jìm-sà-jéui
你　搭　船　去　尖　沙　咀

Néih sìh-sìh daap syùhn heui Jìm-sà-jéui.
你　時　時　搭　船　去　尖　沙　咀　。

SUBSTITUTION DRILLS　(Track 156)

1. Ngóh sīng-kèih-luhk yáuh-sìh fàan-gùng, yáuh-sìh fong-ga.
我　星　期　六　有　時　返　工　，　有　時　放　假　。

a) heui máaih-yéh, hái ūk-kéi 去買嘢，喺屋企

b) sahp-yih-dím fan-gaau, yāt-dím fan-gaau 12:00 瞓覺，1:00 瞓覺

c) heui léuih-hàhng, heui yám-chàh 去旅行，去飲茶

2. Kéuih sìh-sìh tùhng pàhng-yáuh heui <u>yám-chàh</u>.

    佢　時　時　同　朋　友　去　<u>飲　茶</u>　。

    a) léuih-hàhng 旅行　　　　　c) sihk faahn 食飯

    b) máaih-yéh 買嘢

3. Ngóh hóu-síu <u>yám náaih-chàh</u>. 我　好　少　<u>飲　奶　茶</u>　。

    a) tái syù 睇書　　　　　　　c) lohk-yúh chēut heui 落雨出去

    b) fong-ga 放假　　　　　　　d) hái ūk-kéi sihk faahn 喺屋企食飯

REVIEW EXERCISE

I. Rewrite the following sentences

1. léuih-hàhng / ngóh / jó / heui / luhk-yuht

    旅　行　/　我　/　咗　/　去　/　六　月

2. láih-baai-sàam / nī-go / hòi / sei-dím / wúi

    禮　拜　三　/　呢　個　/　開　/　四　點　/　會

3. hóu / kàhm-yaht / hóu-tìn / a / m̀h

    好　/　琴　日　/　好　天　/　呀　/　唔

4. ngóh / daahn-haih / m̀h-dāk-hàahn / dāk-hàahn / sīng-kèih-yih / sīng-kèih-sei

    我　/　但　係　/　唔　得　閒　/　得　閒　/　星　期　二　/　星　期　四

5. hóu m̀h-hóu / a / heui / ngóh-deih / léuih-hàhng / tīng-yaht

    好　唔　好　/　呀　/　去　/　我　哋　/　旅　行　/　聽　日

6. hóu / tìn-hei / ge / gàm-yaht / syù-fuhk

    好　/　天　氣　/　嘅　/　今　日　/　舒　服

II. Translation

1. We seldom go travelling in August.

2. It didn't rain last week.

3. There is a meeting next Monday, but I'm not free to go.

4. Where will you go next Saturday?

5. February is the coldest month.

6. Sometimes I have lunch with my colleagues, sometimes with my friends.

7. The weather was fine on Friday, but it rained on Saturday.

8. I often have lunch in the office.

9. Are we having a holiday on the 23rd of April?

10. I go to work from Monday to Friday. On Saturday, I go shopping. On Sunday, I sleep at home.

11. It was cloudy last Tuesday.

12. The weather in November is very comfortable.

III.   Answer the following questions   (Track 157)

1. Gàm-yaht haih m̀h-haih yàm-tìn a?
   今 日 係 唔 係 陰 天 呀 ？

2. Néih chāt-yuht fong-m̀h-fong ga a?
   你 七 月 放 唔 放 假 呀 ？

3. Hái Hèung-góng, bīn-géi-go-yuht (*which months) yiht a?
   喺 香 港 ， 邊 幾 個 月 熱 呀 ？

4. Néih seuhng go láih-baai-yaht heui-jó bīn-douh a?
   你 上 個 禮 拜 日 去 咗 邊 度 呀 ？

5. Lohk-yúh fàan-gùng haih m̀h-haih hóu màh-fàahn a?
   落 雨 返 工 係 唔 係 好 麻 煩 呀 ？

6. Bīn-go-yuht ge tìn-hei jeui dung a?
   邊 個 月 嘅 天 氣 最 凍 呀 ？

7. Nī-go yuht ge tìn-hei syū m̀h-syù-fuhk a?
   呢 個 月 嘅 天 氣 舒 唔 舒 服 呀 ？

8. Sīng-kèih-yih hóu síu hòi-wúi àh?
   星 期 二 好 少 開 會 吖 ？

9. Néih sìh-sìh daap síu-bā fàan ūk-kéi àh?
你 時 時 搭 小 巴 返 屋 企 吖 ？

IV. Use the following table and answer the questions *(Track 158)*

	Mon	Tue	Wed	Thu	Fri	Sat	Sun
Last week	31℃	28℃	30℃	28℃	29℃	32℃	27℃
This week	20℃	18℃	19℃	17℃	16℃	18℃	25℃
Next Week	26℃	22℃	23℃	29℃	30℃	33℃	21℃

* Gàm-yaht haih sīng-kèih-sàam. Gàm-yaht sahp-gáu douh (*degree).
今 日 係 星 期 三 。 今 日 十 九 度 。

1. Kàhm-yaht géi-dō douh a?
琴 日 幾 多 度 呀 ？

2. Sīng-kèih-yāt géi-dō douh a?
星 期 一 幾 多 度 呀 ？

3. Seuhng-go láih-baai-luhk géi-dō douh a?
上 個 禮 拜 六 幾 多 度 呀 ？

4. Hah-go láih-baai-yih géi-dō douh a?
下 個 禮 拜 二 幾 多 度 呀 ？

5. Láih-baai-yaht géi-dō douh a?
禮 拜 日 幾 多 度 呀 ？

6. Sīng-kèih-ńgh haih m̀h-haih yih-sahp-gáu douh a?
星 期 五 係 唔 係 二 十 九 度 呀 ？

7. Seuhng-go sīng-kèih hóu yiht, haih m̀h-haih a?
上 個 星 期 好 熱 ， 係 唔 係 呀 ？

8. Hah-go sīng-kèih-sei haih m̀h-haih yih sahp douh a?
下 個 星 期 四 係 唔 係 二 十 度 呀 ？

9. Tīng-yaht géi-dō douh a?
聽 日 幾 多 度 呀 ？

10. Hah-go láih-baai dung m̀h-dung a?
下 個 禮 拜 凍 唔 凍 呀 ？

V. Use the given information and answer the questions *(Track 159)*

Sun	Mon	Tue	Wed	Thu	Fri	Sat
				1 ☀	2 ☀	3 ☁
4 ☁	5 ☁	6 ☔	7 ☀	8 ☀	9 ☀	10 ☀
11 ☁	12 ☔	13 ☔	14 ☔	15 ☔	16 ☁	17 ☁
18 ☀	19 ☀	20 ☀	21 ☀	22 ☁	23 ☔	24 ☁
25 ☁	26 ☁	27 ☀	28 ☀	29 ☀	30 ☔	

* Gàm-yaht haih yah-yih houh, yàm-tìn.
今 日 係 廿 二 號 ， 陰 天 。

1. Sīng-kèih-yāt hóu m̀h-hóu-tìn a?
星 期 一 好 唔 好 天 呀 ？

2. Sīng-kèih-yih yáuh móuh lohk-yúh a?
星 期 二 有 冇 落 雨 呀 ？

3. Sahp-sàam-houh haih m̀h-haih yàm-tìn a?
十 三 號 係 唔 係 陰 天 呀 ？

4. Chāt-houh dou sahp-houh haih m̀h-haih hóu-tìn a?
七 號 到 十 號 係 唔 係 好 天 呀 ？

5. Seuhng-go láih-baai-sàam haih m̀h-haih yàm-tìn a?
上 個 禮 拜 三 係 唔 係 陰 天 呀 ？

6. Yih-sahp-gáu-houh lohk-yúh àh?
   二 十 九 號 落 雨 吖 ？

7. Yih-sahp-houh tùhng yih-sahp-sei-houh hóu-tìn àh?
   二 十 號 同 二 十 四 號 好 天 吖 ？

8. Yāt-houh yáuh móuh lohk-yúh a?
   一 號 有 冇 落 雨 呀 ？

9. Kàhm-yaht hóu m̀h-hóu-tìn a?
   琴 日 好 唔 好 天 呀 ？

10. Tīng-yaht haih m̀h-haih yàm-tìn a?
    聽 日 係 唔 係 陰 天 呀 ？

LISTENING EXERCISE

Listen to the dialogues and answer the questions *(Track 160)*

1. _____   4. _____   7. _____   10. _____

2. _____   5. _____   8. _____

3. _____   6. _____   9. _____

Location

CONVERSATION

A. Asking an office location *(Track 161)*

 Néih gūng-sī hái bīn a?
你 公 司 喺 邊 呀 ？
Where is your office?

> bīn 邊 : a contraction of 'bīn-douh 邊度' (where)

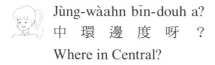 Hái Jùng-wàahn.
喺 中 環 。
It's in Central.

Jùng-wàahn bīn-douh a?
中 環 邊 度 呀 ？
Where in Central?

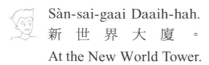 Sàn-sai-gaai Daaih-hah.
新 世 界 大 廈 。
At the New World Tower.

 Káhn m̀h-káhn Ji-deih Gwóng-chèuhng a?
近 唔 近 置 地 廣 場 呀 ？
Is it close to The Landmark?

Hóu káhn. Hái Ji-deih Gwóng-chèuhng deui-mihn.

好 近 。 喺 置 地 廣 場 對 面 。

Very close. It's opposite to The Landmark.

B. Asking how to go to Wan Chai Market *(Track 162)*

Néih sīk mh-sīk heui Wāan-jái gāai-síh a?

你 識 唔 識 去 灣 仔 街 市 呀 ？

Do you know how to go to Wan Chai Market?

Sīk. Ngóh yáuh-sìh heui gó-douh máaih-yéh.

識 。 我 有 時 去 嗰 度 買 嘢 。

I know. I go there to buy things sometime.

Hái nī-douh daap māt-yéh chè heui Wāan-jái gāai-síh jeui faai a?

喺 呢 度 搭 乜 嘢 車 去 灣 仔 街 市 最 快 呀 ？

What is the fastest transport to go to Wan Chai Market (from here)?

Daap bā-sí lā. Hái Hahp-wó Jùng-sàm lohk-chè.

搭 巴 士 啦 。 喺 合 和 中 心 落 車 。

You may take a bus and get off at Hopewell Centre.

Néih jì mh-jì géi-dō houh bā-sí heui Hahp-wó Jùng-sàm a?

你 知 唔 知 幾 多 號 巴 士 去 合 和 中 心 呀 ？

Do you know which bus goes to Hopewell Centre?

Daap sahp-houh bā-sí lā. Bā-sí jaahm hái ngàhn-hòhng chìhn-mihn.

搭 十 號 巴 士 啦 。 巴 士
站 喺 銀 行 前 面 。

You may take bus no. 10. The bus stop is in
front of the bank.

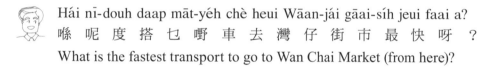

VOCABULARY *(Track 163)*

1. hauh-mihn 後面 / hauh-bihn 後便	PW :	back
2. chìhn-mihn 前面 / chìhn-bihn 前便	PW :	in front
3. seuhng-mihn 上面 / seuhng-bihn 上便	PW :	above; on top of
4. hah-mihn 下面 / hah-bihn 下便	PW :	below; under
5. jó-mihn 左面 / jó-bihn 左便	PW :	left side
6. yauh-mihn 右面 / yauh-bihn 右便	PW :	right side
7. deui-mihn 對面	PW :	opposite side
8. bīn-bihn 邊便 / bīn-mihn 邊面	QW :	which side
9. fuh-gahn 附近	PW :	nearby
10. káhn 近	ADJ :	close to
11. chāan-tēng 餐廳 (M: gàan 間)	N :	restaurant
12. gàai-síh 街市 (M: go 個)	N :	market
13. ngàhn-hòhng 銀行 (M: gàan 間)	N :	bank
14. pou-táu 舖頭 (M: gàan 間)	N :	shop
15. jáu-dim 酒店 (M: gàan 間)	N :	hotel
16. Gwóng-dùng-wá 廣東話	N :	Cantonese
17. Jùng-màhn 中文	N :	Chinese
18. Yīng-màhn 英文	N :	English
19. sīk 識	V :	know how to; have knowledge of; to know (somebody)
20. yùh-gwó 如果	CON :	if
21. jauh 就	CON :	(in case if) ... then
22. síu-síu 少少	ADJ :	a little

SENTENCE PATTERNS

A. Location   *(Track 164)*

1. Ngóh hái chìhn-mihn daap-chè.
   我 喺 前 面 搭 車 。

2. Ngóh hái gàai-síh ge hauh-mihn jyuh, máaih-yéh hóu fòng-bihn.
   我 喺 街 市 嘅 後 面 住 ， 買 嘢 好 方 便 。

3. Deih-tit jaahm ge fuh-gahn yáuh hóu-dò chāan-tēng.
   地 鐵 站 嘅 附 近 有 好 多 餐 廳 。

4. Gó-bún syù hái tói seuhng-mihn.
   嗰 本 書 喺 枱 上 面 。

5. Ngóh jyuh hái néih deui-mihn.
   我 住 喺 你 對 面 。

6. Kéuih séung heui hah-mihn máaih yéh sihk.
   佢 想 去 下 面 買 嘢 食 。

7. Gó-gàan chāan-tēng hái jáu-dim ge yauh-mihn.
   嗰 間 餐 廳 喺 酒 店 嘅 右 面 。

8. Gó-gàan pou-táu ge deui-mihn yáuh bā-sí jaahm.
   嗰 間 舖 頭 嘅 對 面 有 巴 士 站 。

PRACTICE

Translate and answer the questions

1. Where is the phone?

2. Where is the teacher?

3. Where is the hotel that your friends stay?

4. Where is the restaurant that you have dinner?

5. Where is the nearest MTR station?

B. Know : 'sīk' 識 *(Track 165)*

1. Gó-douh yáuh géi-dō go yàhn a? Néih sīk m̀h-sīk kéuih-deih a?
   嗰 度 有 幾 多 個 人 呀 ？ 你 識 唔 識 佢 哋 呀 ？

2. Néih sīk m̀h-sīk Yīng-màhn a? Ngóh sīk síu-síu.
   你 識 唔 識 英 文 呀 ？ 我 識 少 少 。

3. Kéuih sīk m̀h-sīk làih ngóh ūk-kéi a?
   佢 識 唔 識 嚟 我 屋 企 呀 ？

4. Ngóh sīk hàahng heui Gām-jūng deih-tit jaahm.
   我 識 行 去 金 鐘 地 鐵 站 。

5. Ngóh m̀h-sīk tái nī-bún syù.
   我 唔 識 睇 呢 本 書 。

6. Néih sīk m̀h-sīk nī-gàan gūng-sī a?
   你 識 唔 識 呢 間 公 司 呀 ？

7. Kéuih pàhng-yáuh hái Hèung-góng sīk hóu-dò yàhn.
   佢 朋 友 喺 香 港 識 好 多 人 。

8. Ngóh-deih seuhng-go-yuht sīk.
   我 哋 上 個 月 識 。

9. Ngóh sīk síu-síu Jùng-màhn.
   我 識 少 少 中 文 。

10. Ngóh hái Hèung-góng sīk daap-chè, hái Gáu-lùhng (*Kowloon) m̀h-sīk
    我 喺 香 港 識 搭 車 ， 喺 九 龍 唔 識
    daap-chè.
    搭 車 。

Review on 'sīk' 識 and 'jì' 知 *(Track 166)*

☞   sīk + noun / verb
      識 ＋ 名詞/動詞

☞   jì + statement (with a question word)
      知 ＋ 句(常含有疑問詞)

1. Ngóh sīk kéuih.
   我 識 佢 。

2. Ngóh jì kéuih haih bīn-go.
   我 知 佢 係 邊 個 。

3. Ngóh sīk nī-gàan gūng-sī.
   我 識 呢 間 公 司 。

4. Ngóh jì nī-gàan haih māt-yéh gūng-sī.
   我 知 呢 間 係 乜 嘢 公 司 。

5. Kéuih m̀h-sīk fàan ūk-kéi.
   佢 唔 識 返 屋 企 。

6. Kéuih m̀h-jì daap māt-yéh chè fàan ūk-kéi.
   佢 唔 知 搭 乜 嘢 車 返 屋 企 。

PRACTICE

Translate the following into Cantonese

1. I know that there is a restaurant on the 15th floor.

2. He knows my friend.

3. I don't know where the Hang Seng Bank (*Hàhng-sāng Ngàhn-hòhng 恒生銀行) is.

4. I don't know how to go there.

5. I can't read Chinese.

C. If ... then ... : 'yùh-gwó 如果 ... jauh 就 ' *(Track 167)*

1. Néih m̀h làih jauh béi go dihn-wá ngóh lā.
   你 唔 嚟 就 畀 個 電 話 我 啦 。

2. Yùh-gwó jùng-yi jauh máaih lā.
   如 果 鍾 意 就 買 啦 。

3. Yùh-gwó dāk-hàahn jauh yāt-chàih heui sihk faahn lā.
   如 果 得 閒 就 一 齊 去 食 飯 啦 。

4. Yùh-gwó lohk-yúh, fàan-gùng hóu màh-fàahn.
   如 果 落 雨 ， 返 工 好 麻 煩 。

5. Yùh-gwó sīng-kèih-yaht hóu-tìn, ngóh-deih heui bīn-douh wáan a?
   如 果 星 期 日 好 天 ， 我 哋 去 邊 度 玩 呀 ？

PYRAMID DRILLS *(Track 168)*

1.
   daap-chè
   搭 車

   hái chìhn-mihn daap-chè
   喺 前 面 搭 車

   Ngóh hái chìhn-mihn daap-chè
   我 喺 前 面 搭 車

   Ngóh hái jáu-làuh ge chìhn-mihn daap-chè
   我 喺 酒 樓 嘅 前 面 搭 車

2.
   m̀h-hóu chēut heui
   唔 好 出 去

   lohk-yúh m̀h-hóu chēut heui
   落 雨 唔 好 出 去

lohk-yúh jauh m̀h-hóu chēut heui la

落 雨 就 唔 好 出 去 喇

Yùh-gwó lohk-yúh jauh m̀h-hóu chēut heui la.

如 果 落 雨 就 唔 好 出 去 喇 。

SUBSTITUTION DRILLS *(Track 169)*

1. Néih sīk m̀h-sīk Yīng-màhn a?
   你 識 唔 識 英 文 呀 ？

   a) Jūng-màhn 中文

   b) daap-chè fàan ūk-kéi 搭車返屋企

   c) heui deih-tit-jaahm 去地鐵站

   d) Chàhn síu-jé 陳小姐

2. Ngóh jyuh hái néih ge seuhng-mihn.
   我 住 喺 你 嘅 上 面 。

   a) deui-mihn 對面   c) jó-mihn 左面

   b) hauh-mihn 後面   d) fuh-gahn 附近

3. Hah-bihn yáuh ngàhn-hòhng.
   下 便 有 銀 行 。

   a) hóu dò pou-táu 好多舖頭   c) jáu-làuh 酒樓

   b) chāan-tēng 餐廳   d) jáu-dim 酒店

4. Yùh-gwó séung máaih jauh máaih lā.
   如 果 想 買 就 買 啦 。

   a) jùng-yi, sihk dò-dī 鍾意，食多啲

   b) lohk-yúh, m̀h-heui léuih-hàhng 落雨，唔去旅行

   c) néih làih, béi go dihn-wá ngóh 你嚟，畀個電話我

REVIEW EXERCISE

I. Fill in the blanks

1. Ngóh _____ síu-síu Jùng-màhn. Ngóh _____ "yāt", "yih", "sàam",
   "sahp", "yàhn".

   我 _____ 少 少 中 文 。 我 _____ " 一 " 、 " 二 " 、
   " 三 " 、 " 十 " 、 " 人 " 。

2. _____ yáuh chín, ngóh _____ máaih chè.

   _____有 錢 ， 我 _____ 買 車 。

3. Daap _____ heui Gáu-lùhng hóu syù-fuhk.

   搭 _____ 去 九 龍 好 舒 服 。

4. _____ m̀h-syù-fuhk, _____ fàan ūk-kéi lā.

   _____ 唔 舒 服 ， _____ 返 屋 企 啦 。

5. Yùh-gwó hóu gwuih, ngóh _____ .

   如 果 好 劼 ， 我 _____ 。

6. _____ , ngóh jauh tóuh-ngoh.

   _____ ， 我 就 肚 餓 。

II. Translation

1. My colleague lives nearby.

2. I don't know Mr Wong.

3. If you want to buy English books, go to that shop.

4. I know she is Mrs Lee's friend.

5. The door on the left is the way to the market.

6. I'll take a taxi in front of that bank.

7. There are many good restaurants in Central.

8. There are two hotels on the opposite side.

9. His office is behind those shops.

10. There is no minibus (passing by) here.

III. Answer the following questions   *(Track 170)*

1. Néih sīk m̀h-sīk heui daap syùhn a?
   你 識 唔 識 去 搭 船 呀 ？

2. Néih pàhng-yáuh hái bīn-gàan jáu-dim jyuh a?
   你 朋 友 喺 邊 間 酒 店 住 呀 ？

3. Yùh-gwó néih yáuh sahp-maahn mān, néih máaih māt-yéh a?
   如 果 你 有 十 萬 蚊 ， 你 買 乜 嘢 呀 ？

4. Néih ūk-kéi fuh-gahn yáuh móuh gàai-síh a? Néih heui m̀h-heui ga?
   你 屋 企 附 近 有 冇 街 市 呀 ？ 你 去 唔 去 㗎 ？

5. Yùh-gwó tīng-yaht hóu-tìn, néih heui bīn-douh wáan a?
   如 果 聽 日 好 天 ， 你 去 邊 度 玩 呀 ？

6. Sái-sáu-gāan (*toilet) hái bīn-bihn a?
   洗 手 間 喺 邊 便 呀 ？

7. Nī-douh fuh-gahn yáuh géi-dō gàan chāan-tēng a?
   呢 度 附 近 有 幾 多 間 餐 廳 呀 ？

8. Deih-tit jaahm yáuh móuh ngàhn-hòhng a? Yáuh māt-yéh ngàhn-hòhng a?
   地 鐵 站 有 冇 銀 行 呀 ？ 有 乜 嘢 銀 行 呀 ？

9. Néih gūng-sī hah-mihn yáuh móuh pou-táu a?
   你 公 司 下 面 有 冇 舖 頭 呀 ？

10. Néih sīk m̀h-sīk Chàhn sìn-sàang a?
   你 識 唔 識 陳 先 生 呀 ？

IV. Study the map, and answer the questions.   *(Track 171)*

1. Sé-jih-làuh (*office) hái deih-tit jaahm ge bīn-bihn a?
   寫 字 樓 喺 地 鐵 站 嘅 邊 便 呀 ？

2. Bīn-douh yáuh pou-táu a?
   邊 度 有 舖 頭 呀 ？

3. Bīn-douh yáuh gàai-síh a?
   邊 度 有 街 市 呀 ？

4. Bīn-douh yáuh ngàhn-hòhng a?
   邊 度 有 銀 行 呀 ？

5. Sé-jih-làuh ge deui-mihn yáuh móuh jáu-làuh a?
   寫 字 樓 嘅 對 面 有 冇 酒 樓 呀 ？

6. Chāan-tēng hái bīn-douh a?
   餐 廳 喺 邊 度 呀 ？

7. Ngóh séung yám-chàh, heui bīn-douh a?
   我 想 飲 茶 ， 去 邊 度 呀 ？

8. Hái bīn-douh máaih yú a?
   喺 邊 度 買 魚 呀 ？

9. Deih-tit jaahm hái ngàhn-hòhng ge bīn-mihn a?
   地 鐵 站 喺 銀 行 嘅 邊 面 呀 ？

10. Jáu-dim hái bīn-douh a?
    酒 店 喺 邊 度 呀 ？

11. Jáu-dim ge jó-bihn yáuh móuh gàai-síh a?
    酒 店 嘅 左 便 有 冇 街 市 呀 ？

12. Pou-táu hái jáu-làuh ge bīn-bihn a?
    舖 頭 喺 酒 樓 嘅 邊 便 呀 ？

LISTENING EXERCISE

Listen to the dialogues and answer the questions   *(Track 172)*

1. _____	4. _____	7. _____	10. _____
2. _____	5. _____	8. _____	11. _____
3. _____	6. _____	9. _____	12. _____

Lesson 15

Learning Cantonese

CONVERSATION

A. Learning Cantonese *(Track 173)*

Néih jouh-gán māt-yéh a?
你 做 緊 乜 嘢 呀 ？
What are you doing?

Ngóh tái-gán syù.
我 睇 緊 書 。
I am reading a book.

Tái-gán māt-yéh syù a?
睇 緊 乜 嘢 書 呀 ？
What are you reading?

Tái-gán hohk Gwóng-dùng-wá ge syù.
睇 緊 學 廣 東 話 嘅 書 。
I am reading a book on Cantonese.

Néih hohk-gán Gwóng-dùng-wá mē?!
你 學 緊 廣 東 話 咩 ？！
Are you learning Cantonese?

"mē 咩" indicating the mood of surprise

Haih a.

係 呀 。

Yes.

Hohk-jó géi-noih la?

學 咗 幾 耐 喇 ？

How long have you been learning?

Hohk-jó bun nìhn la.

學 咗 半 年 喇 。

I have studied for half a year.

Gwóng-dùng-wá nàahn m̀h-nàahn a?

廣 東 話 難 唔 難 呀 ？

Do you think Cantonese is difficult?

Hóu nàahn.

好 難 。

It is very difficult.

Néih sīk m̀h-sīk góng a?

你 識 唔 識 講 呀 ？

Can you speak (in Cantonese)?

Ngóh sīk góng síu-síu, daahn-haih hóu chā.

我 識 講 少 少 ， 但 係 好 差 。

I can speak a little, but very poorly.

B. How long have you been in H.K.? *(Track 174)*

Néih hái bīn-douh làih ga?

你 喺 邊 度 嚟 㗎 ？

Where are you from?

Ngóh hái Méih-gwok làih.

我 喺 美 國 嚟 。

I came from USA.

Néih làih-jó géi-noih la?
你 嚟 咗 幾 耐 喇 ？
How long have you been here?

Léuhng nìhn la.
兩 年 喇 。
It has been two years.

Néih jùng m̀h-jùng-yi Hèung-góng a?
你 鍾 唔 鍾 意 香 港 呀 ？
Do you like Hong Kong?

Géi jùng-yi lā.
幾 鍾 意 啦 。
I quite like this place.

Yáuh māt-yéh m̀h-gwaan a?
有 乜 嘢 唔 慣 呀 ？
Is there anything you are not used to?

Hèung-góng ge tìn-hei taai yiht, hóu m̀h-syù-fuhk.
香 港 嘅 天 氣 太 熱 ， 好 唔 舒 服 。
The weather in Hong Kong is too hot, it is very uncomfortable.

C. How do you spend your holiday? *(Track 175)*

Hah-go láih-baai fong-ga. Néih wúih heui bīn-douh wáan a?
下 個 禮 拜 放 假 。 你 會 去 邊 度 玩 呀 ？
There is a holiday next week? Where will you go for fun?

Hah-go láih-baai fong-ga mē? Fong māt-yéh ga a?
下 個 禮 拜 放 假 咩 ？ 放 乜 嘢 假 呀 ？
There's a holidday next week? What holiday is it?

Haih Gwok-hing, lìhn-jyuh sīng-kèih-luhk, yaht, fong sàam yaht ga wo.

係 國 慶 ， 連 住 星 期 六 、 日 ， 放 三 日 假 喎 。

It's National Day, joined with Saturday and Sunday, we have three days off!

Haih àh? Dím-gáai ngóh m̀h-jì gé? Néih pìhng-sìh fong-ga heui bīn-douh wáan a?

係 吖 ？ 點 解 我 唔 知 嘅 ？ 你 平 時 放 假 去 邊 度 玩 呀 ？

Really? Why I didn't know about that? Where do you usually go to spent your holidays?

Ngóh tùhng ūk-kéi-yàhn heui Sàm-jan.

我 同 屋 企 人 去 深 圳 。

I go to Shenzhen with my family.

> Shenzhen is the city to the north of Hong Kong

Ngóh dōu séung heui Sàm-jan. Yāt-chàih heui hóu m̀h-hóu a?

我 都 想 去 深 圳 。 一 齊 去 好 唔 好 呀 ？

I want to go to Shenzhen too. Shall we go together?

Hóu a. Yāt-jahn sihk faahn, ngóh-deih kìng-háh lā.

好 呀 。 一 陣 食 飯 ， 我 哋 傾 吓 啦 。

Yes. Let's talk about that at lunch later?

VOCABULARY (Track 176)

1. nìhn or lìhn 年   TW : year

   eg. gauh-nín or gauh-lín 舊年, seuhng-nín or seuhng-lín 上年 : last year (literally old year)

   gàm-nín or gàm-lín /gàm-nìhn or gàm-lìhn 今年 : this year

chēut-nín or chēut-lín 出年, hah-nín or hah-lín 下年：next year
(literally the year out)
yih-lìhng-yāt-lìhng-nìhn 二〇一〇年：Year 2010

2. yaht 日	TW :	day
3. jùng-tàuh 鐘頭 (M: go 個)	TW :	hour
4. fàn-jùng 分鐘	TW :	minute (time spent)
5. géi-noih or géi-loih 幾耐	QW :	how long (time spent)
6. noih or loih 耐	ADJ :	long time
7. yāt-jahn 一陣	TW :	a moment
8. pìhng-sìh 平時	TW :	usually; normally
9. hohk 學	V :	learn
10. góng 講	V :	to speak
11. kìng 傾	V :	to chat; to discuss
12. nám or lám 諗	V :	think
13. wáan 玩	V :	have fun; play
14. wúih 會	AV :	will probably, will
15. verb + gán 緊	VS :	indicating an action under progress

SENTENCE PATTERNS

A. Action under progress   *(Track 177)*

Affirmative statement
☞ hái-douh + verb + gán + object
喺度 ＋ 動詞 ＋ 緊 ＋ 名詞

eg. Kéuih hái- douh tái- gán syù.

佢 喺 度 睇 緊 書 。

He is reading.

Negative statement

☞ m̀h-haih + verb + gán + object

唔係 + 動詞 + 緊 + 名詞

eg. Kéuih m̀h-haih tái- gán syù.

佢 唔 係 睇 緊 書 。

He is not reading.

Question form

☞ haih m̀h-haih + verb + gán + object + a?

係唔係 + 動詞 + 緊 + 名詞 + 呀 ？

eg. Kéuih haih m̀h-haih tái- gán syù a?

佢 係 唔 係 睇 緊 書 呀 ？

Is he reading?

Answer : Haih. / M̀h-haih.

係 。 / 唔 係 。

Yes. / No.

1. Kéuih daap-gán dīk-sí làih nī-douh.

佢 搭 緊 的 士 嚟 呢 度 。

2. Ngóh sihk-gán faahn, m̀h-séung kìng dihn-wá. Ngóh yāt-jahn béi dihn-wá néih.

我 食 緊 飯 ， 唔 想 傾 電 話 。 我 一 陣 畀 電 話 你 。

3. Kéuih hái deih-tit jaahm dáng-gán pàhng-yáuh.

佢 喺 地 鐵 站 等 緊 朋 友 。

4. Néih hái-douh jouh-gán māt-yéh a?

你 喺 度 做 緊 乜 嘢 呀 ？

5. Ngóh hái jáu-làuh tùhng ūk-kéi yàhn (*family) yám-gán chàh.

我 喺 酒 樓 同 屋 企 人 飲 緊 茶 。

6. Kéuih tùhng tùhng-sih hái-douh kìng-gán māt-yéh a?

佢 同 同 事 喺 度 傾 緊 乜 嘢 呀 ？

7. Ngóh nám-gán sàu-gùng heui bīn-douh wáan.

我 諗 緊 收 工 去 邊 度 玩 。

8. Kéuih fàan-gán gùng, m̀h-hái ūk-kéi.

佢 返 緊 工 ， 唔 喺 屋 企 。

9. Ngóh-deih m̀h-haih góng-gán néih.

我 哋 唔 係 講 緊 你 。

10. Néih haih m̀h-haih hohk-gán Gwóng-dùng-wá a?

你 係 唔 係 學 緊 廣 東 話 呀 ？

B. Time spent (Time how long?)

(I)　　(Track 178)

sàam fàn-jùng 三分鐘	3 minutes
yāt go jùng-tàuh 一個鐘頭	1 hour
bun go jùng-tàuh 半個鐘頭	0.5 hour
léuhng yaht 兩日	2 days
yāt go láih-baai/yāt go sīng-kèih	1 week
一個禮拜/一個星期	
chāt go yuht 七個月	7 months
léuhng nìhn 兩年	2 years

PRACTICE

Read the following terms in Cantonese

1. 4 weeks
2. 36 minutes
3. 9 hours
4. 10 days
5. 7 years

6. 500 days
7. 8 months
8. 30 minutes
9. 24 weeks
10. half day

11. 2 hours 20 minutes
12. 6 hours
13. half year
14. 15 months
15. 80 days

(II)   *(Track 179)*

Time spent

☞ Subject + point of time + place + verb + time spent
主語 + 時間詞 + 地方 + 動詞 + 所需時間

eg. Ngóh kàhm-yaht dáng-jó néih yāt go jùng-tàuh.
我 琴 日 等 咗 你 一 個 鐘 頭 。
I waited for you an hour yesterday.

Question form

☞ verb + (yiu) géi-noih a?
動詞 + （要）幾耐呀？

eg. Nī-douh heui Tùhng-lòh-wāan yiu géi-noih a?
呢 度 去 銅 鑼 灣 要 幾 耐 呀 ？
How long does it takes to go to Causeway Bay?

1. Kéuih làih-jó léuhng go láih-baai.
佢 嚟 咗 兩 個 禮 拜 。

2. Ngóh heui gó-douh sahp yih yaht.
我 去 嗰 度 十 二 日 。

3. Kéuih gàm-yaht hái Jùng-wàahn hàahng-jó (*walk) hóu noih.
   佢 今 日 喺 中 環 行 咗 好 耐 。

4. Ngóh tùhng kéuih kìng-jó yāt-jahn dihn-wá.
   我 同 佢 傾 咗 一 陣 電 話 。

5. Néih daap-jó géi-noih chè làih a?
   你 搭 咗 幾 耐 車 嚟 呀 ？

6. Néih hàahng-louh fàan ūk-kéi yiu géi-noih a?
   你 行 路 返 屋 企 要 幾 耐 呀 ？

7. Kéuih hái nī-gàan gūng-sī jouh-jó (*work) sàam nìhn.
   佢 喺 呢 間 公 司 做 咗 三 年 。

8. Ngóh hohk-jó Gwóng-dùng-wá bun nìhn la.
   我 學 咗 廣 東 話 半 年 喇 。

9. Néih nám-jó géi-noih a? Ngóh nám-jó léuhng yaht.
   你 諗 咗 幾 耐 呀 ？ 我 諗 咗 兩 日 。

10. Nī-bún syù máaih-jó géi-noih la?
    呢 本 書 買 咗 幾 耐 喇 ？

11. Kéuih hái Wāan-jái jyuh-jó sei go yuht la.
    佢 喺 灣 仔 住 咗 四 個 月 喇 。

12. Néih làih-jó Hèung-góng géi-noih a?
    你 嚟 咗 香 港 幾 耐 呀 ？

C. Will probably, will : 'wúih' 會 *(Track 180)*

Affirmative statement

☞ wúih + verb
會 + 動詞

eg. Ngóh wúih dáng néih.
我 會 等 你 。
I will wait for you.

Negative statement

☞ m̀h-wúih + verb

　　唔會 + 動詞

eg. Ngóh m̀h-wúih dáng néih.

　　我 唔 會 等 你 。

　　I will not wait for you.

Question form

☞ wúih m̀h-wúih + verb

　　會唔會 + 動詞

eg. Néih wúih m̀h-wúih dáng ngóh a?

　　你 會 唔 會 等 我 呀 ?

　　Will you wait for me?

1. Néih cheut-nín wúih heui bīn-douh léuih-hàhng a?

　　你 出 年 會 去 邊 度 旅 行 呀 ?

2. Néih pàhng-yáuh géi-sìh wúih làih Hèung-góng a?

　　你 朋 友 幾 時 會 嚟 香 港 呀 ?

3. Ngóh chāt-yuht wúih fong-ga.

　　我 七 月 會 放 假 。

4. Tīng-yaht wúih m̀h-wúih hóu-tìn a?

　　聽 日 會 唔 會 好 天 呀 ?

5. Ngóh m̀h-wúih tùhng kéuih yíng-séung.

　　我 唔 會 同 佢 影 相 。

6. Néih-deih yih-sahp houh wúih m̀h-wúih hòi-wúi a?

　　你 哋 二 十 號 會 唔 會 開 會 呀 ?

7. Ngóh hah-go sīng-kèih wúih séuhng-tòhng.

　　我 下 個 星 期 會 上 堂 。

8. Ngóh dāk-hàahn wúih tùhng pàhng-yáuh yám-chàh.
   我　得　閒　會　同　朋　友　飲　茶　。

PRACTICE

Translate and answer the questions

1. Will you have dinner in Admiralty?

2. Will the weather be fine next week?

3. Will you go shopping with your friends next Saturday?

4. What time will you be home tomorrow?

5. Who will you travel with?

6. When shall we have a meeting?

PYRAMID DRILLS　　*(Track 181)*

1.
　　　　　　　　　　māt-yéh a?
　　　　　　　　　乜　嘢　呀　?

　　　　　　　　kìng māt-yéh a?
　　　　　　　　傾　乜　嘢　呀　?

　　　　　　　kìng-gán māt-yéh a?
　　　　　　　傾　緊　乜　嘢　呀　?

　　　　　hái douh kìng-gán māt-yéh a?
　　　　　喺　度　傾　緊　乜　嘢　呀　?

　　　Kéuih hái douh kìng-gán māt-yéh a?
　　　佢　喺　度　傾　緊　乜　嘢　呀　?

Kéuih tùhng pàhng-yáuh hái douh kìng-gán māt-yéh a?
佢　同　朋　友　喺　度　傾　緊　乜　嘢　呀　?

2.

hóu-tìn

好 天

wúih hóu-tìn

會 好 天

m̀h-wúih hóu-tìn

唔 會 好 天

wúih m̀h-wúih hóu-tìn

會 唔 會 好 天

Sīng-kèih-yaht wúih m̀h-wúih hóu-tìn a?

星 期 日 會 唔 會 好 天 呀 ？

3.

léuhng go jùng-tàuh

兩 個 鐘 頭

dáng-jó néih léuhng go jùng-tàuh

等 咗 你 兩 個 鐘 頭

hái chāan-tēng dáng-jó néih léuhng go jùng-tàuh

喺 餐 廳 等 咗 你 兩 個 鐘 頭

Ngóh hái chāan-tēng dáng-jó néih léuhng go jùng-tàuh.

我 喺 餐 廳 等 咗 你 兩 個 鐘 頭 。

Ngóh sīng-kèih-yāt hái chāan-tēng dáng-jó néih léuhng go jùng-tàuh.

我 星 期 一 喺 餐 廳 等 咗 你 兩 個 鐘 頭 。

SUBSTITUTION DRILLS (Track 182)

1. Ngóh làih-jó Hèung-góng léuhng-go láih-baai.

我 嚟 咗 香 港 兩 個 禮 拜 。

a) sei nìhn 四年

b) gáu go yuht 九個月

c) yih sahp ńgh yaht 二十五日

d) chāt go sīng-kèih 七個星期

2. Ngóh hái jáu-dim <u>sihk-gán faahn</u>.

我 喺 酒 店 <u>食</u> 緊 <u>飯</u> 。

   a) yám chàh 飲茶   c) hòi-wúi 開會

   b) dáng pàhng-yáuh 等朋友   d) yíng-séung 影相

3. Kéuih baat-yuht m̀h-wúih <u>fong-ga</u>.

佢 八 月 唔 會 <u>放 假</u> 。

   a) heui léuih-hàhng 去旅行   c) làih Hèung-góng 嚟香港

   b) hòi-wúi 開會   d) hóu-mòhng 好忙

REVIEW EXERCISE

I. Translation

1. My friends will learn Cantonese.

2. What are you doing?

3. I am busy. I'll talk to you later.

4. How long have you been waiting for me?

5. I've been here for 3 years.

6. Who are you talking to?

7. How long does it take you to have lunch?

8. How long ago did you buy this TV set?

9. Usually when you have free time, what will you do?

10. I thought about that for one minute.

11. Will it rain on Friday?

12. I will go to Tsim Sha Tsui shopping on Sunday. Are you coming?

II. Answer the following questions *(Track 183)*

1. Néih dāk-hàahn jouh māt-yéh a ?
   你 得 閒 做 乜 嘢 呀 ？

2. Néih sīng-kèih-luhk wúih heui bīn-douh a?
   你 星 期 六 會 去 邊 度 呀 ？

3. Néih pìhng-sìh dáng pàhng-yáuh, dáng géi-noih a?
   你 平 時 等 朋 友 ， 等 幾 耐 呀 ？

4. Néih gàm-máahn wúih m̀h-wúih béi dihn-wá ngóh a?
   你 今 晚 會 唔 會 畀 電 話 我 呀 ？

5. Néih pìhng-sìh yāt-dím jouh-gán māt-yéh a?
   你 平 時 一 點 做 緊 乜 嘢 呀 ？

6. Néih hohk-gán Gwóng-dùng-wá àh? Hohk-jó géi-noih a?
   你 學 緊 廣 東 話 吖 ？ 學 咗 幾 耐 呀 ？

7. Néih pìhng-sìh daap-chè fàan-gùng yiu géi-noih a?
   你 平 時 搭 車 返 工 要 幾 耐 呀 ？

8. Kéuih tùhng bīn-go góng-gán dihn-wá a?
   佢 同 邊 個 講 緊 電 話 呀 ？

9. Nī-douh heui Jùng-wàahn yiu géi-noih a? Daap māt-yéh chè jeui faai a?
   呢 度 去 中 環 要 幾 耐 呀 ？ 搭 乜 嘢 車 最 快 呀 ？

10. Néih hái Hèung-góng jyuh-jó géi-noih la?
    你 喺 香 港 住 咗 幾 耐 喇 ？

III. Review on 'yih' 二 and 'léuhng' 兩

1. 2 weeks
2. 2:10
3. 2nd of January
4. 2 hours 20 minutes
5. $2.20

9. 22 people
10. 2 cups of tea
11. $2
12. 2,000 books
13. 2 / 2 / 2012

6. next Tuesday

7. 220 books

8. $22,222

14. 202 minutes

15. 212 months

16. 200 years

IV. From the dairy of Mrs Chan, answer the following questions.

(Track 184)

	last week	*this week*	*next week*
Mon	8:00-9:00 Chinese class	3:00 have tea with friends	buy a computer in Mong Kok
Tue	12:30 lunch with Mr. Lee	4:00-6:30 gym	5:30-6:30 Chinese class
Wed	7:45 dinner in Causeway Bay	buy some books in Tsim Sha Tsui	7:00-8:20 play tennis in Admiralty
Thu		12:45-3:00 office lunch meeting	buy a jacket in Wan Chai
Fri	5:30-7:00 swimming	have a drink with colleagues	2:00-4:00 Seminar
Sat	12:20 see a movie	6:00-7:00 Chinese class	
Sun		9:00 hiking in Sai Kung	reading at home

1. Kéuih géi-sìh heui Jìm-Sā-Jéui a? Heui Wāan-Jái nē?
   佢 幾 時 去 尖 沙 咀 呀 ? 去 灣 仔 呢 ?

2. Kéuih nī go sīng-kèih-yāt tùhng bīn-go yāt-chàih a?
   佢 呢 個 星 期 一 同 邊 個 一 齊 呀 ?

3. Kéuih seuhng-go sīng-kèih-luhk jouh māt-yéh a?
   佢 上 個 星 期 六 做 乜 嘢 呀 ?

4. Hah-go sīng-kèih-sāam, kéuih hái bīn-douh a?
下 個 星 期 三 ， 佢 喺 邊 度 呀 ？

5. Kéuih nī-go sīng-kèih-yaht heui m̀h heui wáan a?
佢 呢 個 星 期 日 去 唔 去 玩 呀 ？

6. Kéuih sīng-kèih-ńgh tùhng bīn-go heui yám yéh a?
佢 星 期 五 同 邊 個 飲 嘢 呀 ？

7. Kéuih yāt go sīng-kèih hohk Jùng-màhn géi-dò go jùng-tauh a?
佢 一 個 星 期 學 中 文 幾 多 個 鐘 頭 呀 ？

8. Nī-go sīng-kèih-sei, kéuih hái bīn-douh sihk faahn a?
呢 個 星 期 四 ， 佢 喺 邊 度 食 飯 呀 ？

9. Kéuih seuhng-go sīng-kèih-yih tùhng bīn-go sihk faahn a?
佢 上 個 星 期 二 同 邊 個 食 飯 呀 ？

Géi dím sihk a?
幾 點 食 呀 ？

10. Kéuih hah-go sīng-kèih-yaht hái ūk-kéi jouh māt-yéh a?
佢 下 個 星 期 日 喺 屋 企 做 乜 嘢 呀 ？

Lesson 16

Tour around Hong Kong

CONVERSATION

A. Chinese food in Hong Kong *(Track 185)*

Néih heui-gwo Sài-gung sihk hói-sìn meih a?

你　去　過　西　貢　食　海　鮮　未　呀　？

Have you been to Sai Kung to eat seafood?

Heui-gwo.　Ngóh tùhng Hèung-góng pàhng-yáuh heui sihk-gwo géi chi la.

去　過　。　我　同　香　港　朋　友　去　食　過　幾　次　喇　。

Yes. I've been there with my Hong Kong friends a few times.

Néih jùng m̀h-jùng-yi sihk a?

你　鍾　唔　鍾　意　食　呀　？

Do you like it?

Hóu jùng-yi. Hèung-góng ge hói-sìn hóu hóu-sihk. Ngóh dōu hóu jùng-yi heui yám-chàh.

好　鍾　意　。　香　港　嘅　海　鮮　好　好　食　。　我　都　好　鍾　意　去　飲　茶　。

Yes. The seafood in Hong Kong is very tasty. I also like to go for dim sum.

Néih jeui jùng-yi sihk māt-yéh dím-sām a?

你 最 鍾 意 食 乜 嘢 點 心 呀 ?

What is your favourite dim sum?

Ngóh jeui jùng-yi sihk hà-gáau tùhng chā-sīu-bāau.

我 最 鍾 意 食 蝦 餃 同 叉 燒 包 。

I like shrimp dumpling and BBQ pork bun the most.

B. Have your family ever been to Hong Kong? *(Track 186)*

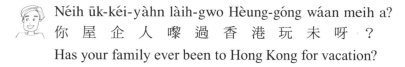

Néih ūk-kéi-yàhn làih-gwo Hèung-góng wáan meih a?

你 屋 企 人 嚟 過 香 港 玩 未 呀 ?

Has your family ever been to Hong Kong for vacation?

Ngóh bàh-bā màh-mā gauh-nín làih-gwo.

我 爸 爸 媽 媽 舊 年 嚟 過 。

My father and mother came here last year.

Làih jó géi-noih a?

嚟 咗 幾 耐 呀 ?

How long did they stay?

Làih-jó yāt go yuht dóu.

嚟 咗 一 個 月 倒 。

Approximately one month.

Néih tùhng kéuih-deih heui-gwo bīn-douh wáan a?

你 同 佢 哋 去 過 邊 度 玩 呀 ?

Where did you take them to?

Ngóh-deih heui gwo Sàan-déng, Chek-chyúh, tùhng-màaih hái Wohng-gok máaih yéh.

我 哋 去 過 山 頂 、 赤 柱 , 同 埋 喺 旺 角 買 嘢 。

We have been to the Peak, Stanley, and went shopping in Mong Kok.

Kéuih-deih hòi m̀h-hòi-sàm a?

佢 哋 開 唔 開 心 呀 ？

Did they have fun?

Kéuih-deih hóu hòi-sàm. Ngóh bàh-bā wah juhng yiu làih hóu dò chi.

佢 哋 好 開 心 。 我 爸 爸 話 仲 要 嚟 好 多 次 。

They were happy, and my father said he would like to come many times.

C. Going to see a movie *(Track 187)*

Néih tái-gwo Hèung-góng ge hei meih a?

你 睇 過 香 港 嘅 戲 未 呀 ？

Have you ever seen any Hong Kong films?

Meih tái-gwo.

未 睇 過 。

No, I haven't.

Yìh-gā yáuh tou hóu hóu-tái ge hei. Ngóh séung chéng néih tái.

而 家 有 套 好 好 睇 嘅 戲 。 我 想 請 你 睇 。

There is a very good movie on show, I want to take you to see it.

Dò-jeh sin. Ngóh-deih géi-sìh heui tái a?

多 謝 先 。 我 哋 幾 時 去 睇 呀 ？

Thank you (in advance). When shall we go?

Néih tīng-máahn dāk m̀h-dāk-hàahn a?

你 聽 晚 得 唔 得 閒 呀 ？

Are you free tomorrow evening?

Dāk-hàahn. Ngóh-deih tīng-máahn heui tái lā.

得 閒 。 我 哋 聽 晚 去 睇 啦 。

Yes. Let's go to see it tomorrow evening.

Hóu a. Néih luhk-dím jáu-dāk meih a?

好 呀 。 你 六 點 走 得 未 呀 ？

OK. Can you leave the office at 6:00?

Ngóh luhk-dím meih jáu-dāk. Luhk-dím-bun lā, hóu m̀h-hóu a?

我 六 點 未 走 得 。 六 點 半 啦 ， 好 唔 好 呀 ？

I can't leave at 6:00. What about 6:30?

Hóu. Ngóh-deih heui sihk faahn sìn, jì-hauh heui tái hei lā.

好 。 我 哋 去 食 飯 先 ， 之 後 去 睇 戲 啦 。

OK. We will have dinner first, and then go to the movie.

VOCABULARY   (Track 188)

1. chi 次	N :	occasion, times
2. verb + gwo 過	VS :	indicating experiences
3. meih 未	P :	not yet
4. verb + dāk 得	V/VS :	allow to, can, O.K.
5. sìn 先	ADV :	first
6. jì-hauh 之後	TW :	afterwards; later on
7. wáan 玩	V :	have fun; play
eg. hóu-wáan 好玩 : good fun		
8. gin 見	V :	meet
9. Yaht-bún choi 日本菜	N :	Japanese cuisine
* Jùng-gwok choi 中國菜: Chinese cuisine		
* Taai-gwok choi 泰國菜: Thai cuisine		
* Yuht-nàahm choi 越南菜: Vietnamese cuisine		
* Hòhn-gwok choi 韓國菜 : Korean cuisine		
* Yi-daaih-leih choi 意大利菜: Italian cuisine		
* Faat-gwok choi 法國菜: French cuisine		
10. tèng 聽	V :	listen; hear
11. chéng 請	V :	invite; treat

12. jáu 走   V : leave
13. laaht 辣   ADJ : hot and spicy
   * tìhm 甜 : sweet
   * hàahm 鹹 : salty
   * syùn 酸 : sour
   * fú 苦 : bitter

SENTENCE PATTERNS

A. Showing one's experience *(Track 189)*

Affirmative statement

☞ verb + gwo

動詞 ＋ 過

eg. Néih heui-gwo ngóh ūk-kéi.

你 去 過 我 屋 企 。

You've been to my house.

Negative statement

☞ móuh + verb + gwo

冇 ＋ 動詞 ＋ 過

eg. Néih móuh heui-gwo ngóh ūk-kéi.

你 冇 去 過 我 屋 企 。

You've never been to my house.

Question form

☞ yáuh móuh + verb + gwo + object + a?

有冇 ＋ 動詞 ＋ 動詞 ＋ 過 ＋ 名詞 ＋ 呀？

eg. Néih yáuh móuh heui-gwo ngóh ūk-kéi a?

你 有 冇 去 過 我 屋 企 呀 ？

Have you ever been to my house?

Answer : Yáuh. / Móuh.

有 。 ／ 冇 。

Yes. / No.

1. Néih yáuh móuh heuiògwo Sàan-déng yíng-séung a?
   你 有 冇 去 過 山 頂 影 相 呀 ？

2. Ngóh-deih sihk-gwo Yaht-bún choi géi chi.
   我 哋 食 過 日 本 菜 幾 次 。

3. Kéuih gauh-nín làih-gwo Hèung-góng.
   佢 舊 年 嚟 過 香 港 。

4. Ngóh gàm-yaht móuh yám-gwo chàh.
   我 今 日 冇 飲 過 茶 。

5. Ngóh pàhng-yáuh móuh làih-gwo séuhng-tòhng.
   我 朋 友 冇 嚟 過 上 堂 。

6. Néih yáuh móuh heui-gwo Dihk-sih-nèih (*Disneyland) wáan a?
   你 有 冇 去 過 迪 士 尼 玩 呀 ？

7. Kéuih móuh hohk-gwo Gwóng-dùng-wá, sīk tèng m̀h-sīk góng.
   佢 冇 學 過 廣 東 話 ， 識 聽 唔 識 講 。

8. Seuhng-go láih-baai yáuh móuh hòi-gwo wúi a?
   上 個 禮 拜 有 冇 開 過 會 呀 ？

9. Ngóh kàhm-máahn móuh fan-gwo gaau.
   我 琴 晚 冇 瞓 過 覺 。

10. Ngóh daap-gwo síu-bā làih nī-douh, daahn-haih móuh daap-gwo bā-sí
    我 搭 過 小 巴 嚟 呢 度 ， 但 係 冇 搭 過 巴 士
    làih.
    嚟 。

PRACTICE

Translate and answer the questions

1. Have you seen this movie before?

2. Have you learned Chinese before?

3. Have you been to that restaurant?

4. Did you talk to him?

5. Did you sleep last night? How many hours did you sleep?

6. Have you ever stayed in the Hong Kong Hotel in Tsim Sha Tsui?

B. Not yet : 'meih' 未   *(Track 190)*

Negative statement

☞ meih + verb + (gwo)
未 ＋ 動詞 ＋（過）

eg. Néih meih sihk faahn.
你 未 食 飯 。
You haven't eat yet.

Néih meih heui-gwo ngóh ūk-kéi.
你 未 去 過 我 屋 企 。
You've never been to my house.

Question form

☞ verb (jó/gwo) + object + meih a?
動詞（咗/過）＋ 名詞 ＋ 未呀？

eg. Néih sihk-jó faahn meih a?
你 食 咗 飯 未 呀 ？
Have you eaten yet?

Answer : Sihk-jó la. / Meih sihk.

食 咗 喇 。 / 未 食 。

Yes. / No.

Néih heui-gwo ngóh ūk-kéi meih a?

你 去 過 我 屋 企 未 呀 ？

Have you ever been to my house?

Answer : Heui-gwo la. / Meih heui-gwo.

去 過 喇 。 / 未 去 過 。

Yes. / No.

1. Néih gin-gwo Wòhng sàang meih a?
   你 見 過 黃 生 未 呀 ？

2. Ngóh m̀h-dāk-hàahn, nī-go yuht dōu meih béi-gwo dihn-wá kéuih.
   我 唔 得 閒 ， 呢 個 月 都 未 畀 過 電 話 佢 。

3. Kéuih gàm-yaht meih sihk-gwo yéh.
   佢 今 日 未 食 過 嘢 。

4. Néih pàhng-yáuh dou-jó meih a?
   你 朋 友 到 咗 未 呀 ？

5. Léih síu-jé meih séuhng-gwo tòhng.
   李 小 姐 未 上 過 堂 。

6. Ngóh gin-gwo kéuih, meih gin-gwo kéuih taai-táai.
   我 見 過 佢 ， 未 見 過 佢 太 太 。

7. Néih-deih hòi-jó wúi meih a?
   你 哋 開 咗 會 未 呀 ？

8. Kéuih meih hohk-gwo Gwóng-dùng-wá, kéuih hóu séung hohk.
   佢 未 學 過 廣 東 話 ， 佢 好 想 學 。

9. Kéuih meih làih, ngóh-deih dáng m̀h-dáng kéuih a?
   佢 未 嚟 ， 我 哋 等 唔 等 佢 呀 ？

PRACTICE

Translate and answer the questions

1. Are you hungry now?

2. Have you had lunch yet?

3. Have you bought that book?

4. Have you called your colleague?

5. Have you gone to the bank?

6. Are you free now? How long do I have to wait?

C. Can or allow to : 'dāk' 得   *(Track 191)*

☞ *Affirmative statement*

verb + dāk

動詞 ＋ 得

eg. Kéuih làih-dāk.

佢　嚟　得　。

He can come.

☞ *Negative statement*

m̀h + verb + dāk

唔 ＋ 動詞 ＋ 得

eg. Kéuih m̀h-làih-dāk.

佢　唔　嚟　得　。

He can't come.

☞ *Question form*

verb + m̀h + verb + dāk + a?

動詞 ＋ 唔 ＋ 動詞 ＋ 得 ＋ 呀 ？

eg. Kéuih làih m̀h-làih dāk a?

佢 嚟 唔 嚟 得 呀 ？

Can he come?

Answer : Làih-dāk. / M̀h-làih-dāk

嚟 得 。 / 唔 嚟 得 。

Yes. / No.

☞ statement + dāk m̀h-dāk a?

句 + 得 唔 得 呀 ？

eg. Ngóh yìh-gā làih, dāk m̀h-dāk a?

我 而 家 嚟 ， 得 唔 得 呀 ？

May I come now?

Answer : Dāk. / M̀h-dāk.

得 。 / 唔 得 。

Yes. / No.

1. Ngóh tīng-yaht m̀h-dāk-hàahn, m̀h-heui-dāk yám-chàh.
我 聽 日 唔 得 閒 ， 唔 去 得 飲 茶 。

2. Ngóh m̀h-sihk-dāk laaht (ge yéh).
我 唔 食 得 辣 （ 嘅 嘢 ） 。

3. Néih yáuh hóu-dò yéh yiu jouh, néih meih jáu-dāk.
你 有 好 多 嘢 要 做 ， 你 未 走 得 。

4. Nī-douh m̀h-jyun-dāk yauh.
呢 度 唔 轉 得 右 。

5. Ngóh hóu gwuih, m̀h-hàahng-dāk la.
我 好 劫 ， 唔 行 得 喇 。

6. Nī-dī yéh sihk m̀h-sihk-dāk ga?
呢 啲 嘢 食 唔 食 得 㗎 ？

7. Ngóh m̀h-sīk-dāk kéuih. Kéuih haih bīn-go a? Néih gin-gwo kéuih meih
   我 唔 識 得 佢 。 佢 係 邊 個 呀 ？ 你 哋 見 過 佢 未
   a?
   呀 ？

8. Chàhn sìn-sàang gàm-yaht m̀h-fàan-dāk gùng.
   陳 先 生 今 日 唔 返 得 工 。

9. Ngóh m̀h-daap-dāk syùhn. Ngóh daap syùhn jauh m̀h-syù-fuhk.
   我 唔 搭 得 船 。 我 搭 船 就 唔 舒 服 。

10. Ngóh jáu sìn, dāk m̀h-dāk a?
    我 走 先 ， 得 唔 得 呀 ？

11. Faai-dī dāk m̀h-dāk a?
    快 啲 得 唔 得 呀 ？

12. Néih chéng ngóh sihk faahn, dāk m̀h-dāk a?
    你 請 我 食 飯 ， 得 唔 得 呀 ？

PRACTICE

Translate and answer the questions

1. Can we make a left turn there?

2. Can you eat spicy food?

3. Can I call you after 12:00? Are you asleep?

4. Can you drink beer?

D. First : 'sin' 先 (Track 192)

1. M̀h-gòi heui Wāan-jái sìn, jì-hauh heui Tùhng-lòh-wāan.
   唔 該 去 灣 仔 先 ， 之 後 去 銅 鑼 灣 。

2. Néih-deih sihk sìn lā.
   你 哋 食 先 啦 。

3. Néih hàahng sìn lā. Ngóh hàahng néih hauh-bihn.
   你 行 先 啦 。 我 行 你 後 便 。

4. Ngóh jáu sìn la. Tīng-yaht gin.
   我　走　先　喇　。　聽　日　見　。

5. Néih tóuh-ngoh jauh sihk faahn sìn lā.
   你　肚　餓　就　食　飯　先　啦　。

6. Néih dáng ngóh yāt-jahn, ngóh yiu tèng dihn-wá sìn.
   你　等　我　一　陣　，　我　要　聽　電　話　先　。

PYRAMID DRILLS   *(Track 193)*

1.   hohk Gwóng-dùung-wá
                        學　廣　東　話

                    hohk-gwo Gwóng-dùng-wá
                      學　過　廣　東　話

                 móuh hohk-gwo Gwóng-dùng-wá
                   冇　學　過　廣　東　話

              yáuh móuh hohk-gwo Gwóng-dùng-wá a?
                有　冇　學　過　廣　東　話　呀　?

          Néih yáuh móuh hohk-gwo Gwóng-dùng-wá a?
            你　有　冇　學　過　廣　東　話　呀　?

2.   Léih síu-jé
                          李　小　姐

                       gin Léih síu-jé
                        見　李　小　姐

                     gin-gwo Léih síu-jé
                      見　過　李　小　姐

                   meih gin-gwo Léih síu-jé
                    未　見　過　李　小　姐

                Ngóh meih gin-gwo Léih síu-jé.
                 我　未　見　過　李　小　姐　。

3.

béi dihn-wá néih
畀　電　話　你

béi -jó dihn-wá néih
畀　咗　電　話　你

Chàhn táai béi-jó dihn-wá néih
陳　太　畀　咗　電　話　你

Chàhn táai béi-jó dihn-wá néih meih a?
陳　太　畀　咗　電　話　你　未　呀　？

4.

m̀h-fàan-gùng
唔　返　工

m̀h-fàan-dāk gùng
唔　返　得　工

gàm-yaht m̀h-fàan-dāk gùng
今　日　唔　返　得　工

Wòhng sìn-sàang gàm-yaht m̀h-fàan-dāk gùng
王　先　生　今　日　唔　返　得　工

Wòhng sìn-sàang gàm-yaht fàan m̀h-fàan-dāk gùng a?
王　先　生　今　日　返　唔　返　得　工　呀　？

SUBSTITUTION DRILLS　*(Track 194)*

1. Nī-dī dím-sām hóu <u>tìhm</u>.
   呢　啲　點　心　好　<u>甜</u>　。

   a) hàahm 鹹   c) yiht 熱

   b) laaht 辣   d) daaih 大

2. Ngóh meih heui-gwo yám-chàh.
   我　未　去　過　飲　茶　。

   a) hòi wúi 開會

   b) Chek-chyúh 赤柱

   c) sihk Yi-daaih-leih choi 食意大利菜

3. Kéuih gàm-yaht m̀h-dāk-hàahn, kéuih m̀h-heui-dāk yám chàh.
   佢　今　日　唔　得　閒　，　佢　唔　去　得　飲　茶　。

   a) làih-dāk hòi wúi 嚟得開會

   b) fàan-dāk ūk-kéi sihk faahn 返得屋企食飯

   c) tái-dāk dihn-sih 睇得電視

4. M̀h-gòi néih heui Tùhng-lòh-wāan sìn.
   唔　該　你　去　銅　鑼　灣　先　。

   a) yám tòng 飲湯

   b) máaih syù 買書

   c) béi dihn-wá kéuih 畀電話佢

   d) fàan gūng-sī 返公司

REVIEW EXERCISE

I.   Translation

1. Have you ever been to that restaurant to eat dim sum?

2. I remember but I have not done it yet.

3. Have you ever ride on the MTR?

4. I have never been to your house.

5. He is sick. He cannot attend the meeting today.

6. Is this sweet or salty?

7. You eat first. I'm not hungry.

8. I have to answer the phone first. We'll talk later.

9. You cannot go straight here. You have to turn left.

10. I have never met him before. Who is he?

11. She has not go home yet.

12. Did you see that movie? I've seen it twice.

II. Answer the following questiions *(Track 195)*

1. Néih yáuh móuh hái Sùhng-gwòng (*Sogo) máaih-gwo yéh a?

   你 有 冇 喺 崇 光 買 過 嘢 呀 ?

2. Néih yám-gwo lèuhng-chàh (*Chinese herbal tea) meih a?

   你 飲 過 涼 茶 未 呀 ?

3. Néih sihk-gwo Taai-gwok choi meih a? Bīn-gāan chāan-tēng hóu-sihk a?

   你 食 過 泰 國 菜 未 呀 ? 邊 間 餐 廳 好 食 呀 ?

4. Néih chéng ngóh heui yám-chàh dāk m̀h-dāk a? Néih géi-sìh dāk-hàahn a?

   你 請 我 去 飲 茶 得 唔 得 呀 ? 你 幾 時 得 閒 呀 ?

5. Néih yáuh móuh heui-gwo Nàahm-ā Dóu (*Lamma Island) sihk hói-sìn a?

   你 有 冇 去 過 南 丫 島 食 海 鮮 呀 ?

6. Néih yáuh móuh hái Hèung-góng gēi-chèuhng yíng-gwo séung a?

   你 有 冇 喺 香 港 機 場 影 過 相 呀 ?

7. Néih yáuh móuh heui-gwo Hói-yèuhng Gūng-yún (*Ocean Park) a?

   你 有 冇 去 過 海 洋 公 園 呀 ?

8. Pìhng-sìh néih dihng néih taai-táai fàan ūk-kéi sìn a?

   平 時 你 定 你 太 太 返 屋 企 先 呀 ?

9. Néih yáuh móuh hái Sāan-déng jyuh-gwo a?

   你 有 冇 喺 山 頂 住 過 呀 ?

10. Néih gáu-dím hái-douh meih a?

    你 九 點 喺 度 未 呀 ?

III. Translate and the questions.

1. What time do you get up?

2. Do you eat anything in the morning? (*jìu-jóu 朝早 : morning)

3. What time do you go to work?

4. How do you go to the office? Do you go to work by taxi? (*dím-yéung 點樣 : how)

5. Where is your office?

6. Do you work on Saturdays?

7. What time do you have lunch?

8. Where do you often go for lunch?

9. Do you like to eat dim sum?

10. What time do you finish work?

11. What do you say to your colleagues when you leave?

12. What did you do after work yesterday?

13. Do you like to go for a drink with your friends?

14. What time do you   home?

15. What transport do you take to go home?

16. Where do you live? On which floor?

17. What time do you have dinner?

18. Who do you have dinner with?

19. Do you watch TV while eating?

20. When will you go out for dinner?

21. Do you want to have BBQ pork with rice tonight?

22. What time do you go to bed?

23. What do you like to do when you have time?

24. Do you like shopping? Do you usually go to Causeway Bay shopping?

Appendix 1

Cantonese to English

	Lesson		
B			
bā-sí 巴士 (M: ga 架)	3	N :	bus
baahk-sīk 白色	6	N :	white
bāai-baai 拜拜	2	PH :	goodbye
baak 百	6/10	NU :	hundred
baat 八	1	NU :	eight
baat-yuht 八月	4	N :	August
báau 飽	10	ADJ :	full (stomach)
bē-jáu 啤酒	11	N :	beer
béi 畀	7	V :	give
bīn-bihn 邊便	14	QW :	which side
bīn-dī 邊啲	5	QW :	which of these
bīn-douh 邊度	3	QW :	where
bīn-go 邊個	5	QW :	which one; who
bīn-go yuht 邊個月	13	QW :	which month
bīn-mihn 邊面	14	QW :	which side
bīng-séui 冰水	10	N :	ice water
bōng 幫	11	V :	help; assist

būi 杯 (M: jek 隻 / go 個)   7   N :   cup; glass; mug

C

chā 差   15   ADJ :   bad; poor

chàh 茶   10   N :   tea

chà-sìu-bāau 叉燒包   10   N :   BBQ pork bun

chà-sìu faahn 叉燒飯   7   N :   BBQ pork with rice

chāan-tēng 餐廳 (M: gàan 間)   14   N :   restaurant

cháang 橙   7   N :   orange

cháang-sīk 橙色   6   N :   orange colour

chāt 七   1   NU :   seven

chāt-yuht 七月   4   N :   July

Chek-chyúh 赤柱   16   PW :   Stanley

chéng 請   11/16   V :   invite; treat

chéng-mahn 請問   11   PH :   May I ask?

chēut heui 出去   8   PH :   go out

chēut-nín 出年   15   TW :   next year

chi 次   16   N :   occasion, times

chìhn-bihn 前便   14   PW :   in front

chìhn-mihn 前面   3/14   PW :   in front

chín 錢   6   N :   money

chìn 千   10   NU :   thousand

Chīuh-jāu-choi 潮州菜   12   N :   Chiuchow cuisine

choi 菜   11   N :   vegetables

D

dá-fùng 打風   13   N :   typhoon

daaih 大	6	ADJ :	big; large
dāan 單 (M: jèung 張)	11	N :	receipt; bill; invoice
dáan 蛋 (M: jek 隻)	7	N :	egg
daahn-haih 但係	13	CON :	but; however
daap chè 搭車	3/9	VO :	take a car, bus, etc.
dāk 得	2/6/16	V/VS :	O.K.; allow to; can
dāk-hàahn 得閒	9	ADJ :	have free time
dáng 等	10	V :	wait
dáng dáng 等等	2	PH :	wait a moment
dāng-wái 燈位	3	PW :	at the traffic lights
dehng tói 訂枱	11	VO :	reserve table
deih-há 地下	12	PW :	ground floor
deih-tit 地鐵	3	N :	MTR (Mass Transit Railway)
deih-tit jaahm 地鐵站	3	PW :	MTR station
deui-mihn 對面	14	PW :	opposite side
dī 啲 + N	5	M :	indicating plural form or uncountable
ADJ + dī 啲	6	ADV :	a little more
dihn-chè 電車 (M: ga 架)	3	N :	tram
dihn-wá 電話 (M: go 個)	5	N :	telephone
dihng (-haih) 定(係)	7	CON :	or (in a question)
dīk-sí 的士 (M: ga 架)	3	N :	taxi
dím 點	4	TW :	o'clock
dím-gáai 點解	9	QW :	why
dím-sām 點心 (M: go 個)	10	N :	dim sum
dò 多	11	ADJ :	many, much, plenty
dò-dī 多啲	11	PH :	some more

dò-jeh 多謝	2	PH :	thank you
dói 袋 (M: go 個)	6	N :	bag
dōu 都	10	ADV :	also
N + dóu 倒	13/16	P :	approximately
dou 到	13	CON/V :	until; to, arrive
douh 度	13	N :	degree
dung 凍	7	ADJ :	cold
dung séui 凍水	10	N :	cold water

F

faahn 飯	11	N :	rice
faai dī lā 快啲啦	2	PH :	faster please
faai-jí 筷子	11	N :	chopsticks
Faat-gwok choi 法國菜	16	N :	French cuisine
fàan-gùng 返工	8	VO :	go to work
fàan ūk-kéi 返屋企	8	VO :	go home
fan-gaau 瞓覺	8	VO :	sleep
fán-hùhng-sīk 粉紅色	6	N :	pink
fàn-jùng 分鐘	15	TW :	minute (time spent)
fēi-gēi 飛機 (M: ga 架)	3	N :	airplane
fó-téui 火腿	7	N :	ham
fòng-bihn 方便	12	ADJ :	convenient
fong-ga 放假	13	VO :	on holiday
fú 苦	16	ADJ :	bitter
fuh-gahn 附近	14	PW :	nearby
fùi-sīk 灰色	6	N :	grey
fun-yìhng gwòng làhm 歡迎光臨	11	PH :	welcome

G

ga-fē 咖啡	7	N :	coffee
(ga-)fē-sīk (咖)啡色	6	N :	brown
gàai-háu 街口 (M: go 個)	3	PW :	street corner
gàai-síh 街市 (M: go 個)	14	N :	market
gaau 教	3	V :	teach; instruct
gám 咁	12	P :	well
gàm-go láih-baai 今個禮拜	13	TW :	this week
gàm-go sīng-kèih 今個星期	13	TW :	this week
gàm-go yuht 今個月	13	TW :	this month
Gām-jūng 金鐘	12	PW :	Admiralty
gàm-nín 今年	15	TW :	this year
gàm-sīk 金色	6	N :	gold
gàm-yaht 今日	10	TW :	today
(verb) + gán 緊	15	VS :	indicating an action under progress
gáu 九	1	NU :	nine
Gáu-lùhng 九龍	14	PW :	Kowloon
gáu-yuht 九月	4	N :	September
gauh-nín 舊年	15	TW :	last year
ge 嘅	5	P :	indicating modification
géi 幾	9	ADV :	quite
gei-dāk 記得	13	V :	remember
géi(-dō) chín 幾(多)錢	6	QW :	cost how much
géi(-dō)-dím 幾(多)點	4	QW :	what time
géi(-dō) houh 幾(多)號	4	QW :	what number; what date
géi-dō jit? 幾多折？	6	PH :	what's the discount?

hàahng-louh 行路	3	VO :	walk
hah-go láih-baai 下個禮拜	13	TW :	next week
hah-go sīng-kèih 下個星期	13	TW :	next week
hah-go yuht 下個月	13	TW :	next month
hah-bihn 下便	14	PW :	below; under
hah-mihn 下面	14	PW :	below; under
hah-nín 下年	15	TW :	next year
hái 喺	12	P :	located at, in or on
haih 係	5	V :	equals to, verb to be
haih a 係呀	2	PH :	it is true; yeah
hái douh sihk 喺度食	7	PH :	eat here
hahp 盒	7	N/M :	box
hauh-bihn 後便	14	PW :	back
hauh-mihn 後面	14	PW :	back
hei-mohng 希望	13	V :	hope; wish
héi-sàn 起身	8	VO :	get up
heui 去	3	V :	go
Hèung-góng 香港	13	PW :	Hong Kong
hó-lohk 可樂	7/6	N :	coke
hohk 學	15	V :	learn
Hòhn-gwok choi 韓國菜	16	N :	Korean cuisine
hòi-chí 開始	13	V :	begin
hòi-sàm 開心	10	ADJ :	happy
hòi-wúi 開會	13	VO :	to hold a meeting
hói-sìn 海鮮	16	N :	seafood
hóu 好	6	ADV :	very
		ADJ :	good; fine
hóu dò 好多	11	PH :	plenty, a lot, many

hóu noih móuh gin 好耐冇見	5	PH :	Haven't seen you for a long time
hóu síu 好少	13	ADV :	rarely, seldom
hóu-sihk 好食	10	ADJ :	delicious
hóu-tái 好睇	16	ADJ :	interesting; good looking
hóu-tìn 好天	13	ADJ :	fine weather
hóu-wáan 好玩	16	ADJ :	good fun
houh 號	4/10	TW :	day (of a month), number
houh-jí 毫子	6	N :	ten cents
hùhng-sīk 紅色	6	N :	red

J

jà-chè 揸車	3	V :	drive
jàn-haih 真係	12	ADV :	really
jáu 走	9/16	V :	leave, run
jáu-dim 酒店 (M: gàan 間)	14	N :	hotel
jáu-làuh 酒樓 (M: gàan 間)	12	N :	Chinese restaurant
jauh 就	14	CON :	(in case if) ... then
jeui 最	13	P :	most
jì 知	13	V :	to know (a fact)
jì-hauh 之後	9/16	TW :	afterwards; later on
jí-sīk 紫色	6	N :	purple
jihk heui 直去	3	PH :	go straight
Jìm-sà-jéui 尖沙咀	12	PW :	Tsim Sha Tsui
jit 折	6	N :	discount
V + jó 咗	11	VS :	indicating completion
jó-bihn 左便	14	PW :	left side
jó-mihn 左面	14	PW :	left side

joi-gin 再見	3	PH : see you
jóu-sàhn 早晨	2	PH : Good morning
jouh 做	7	V : to do
Jùng-gwok choi 中國菜	16	N : Chinese cuisine
Jùng-màhn 中文	14	N : Chinese
jùng-tàuh 鐘頭 (M: go 個)	15	TW : hour
Jùng-wàahn 中環	3	PW : Central
Jùng-wàahn Gwóng-chèuhng 中環廣場	12	PW : Central Plaza
jùng-yi 鍾意	10	V/AV : like
jyuh 住	12	V : live
jyun jó 轉左	3	VO : turn left
jyun yauh 轉右	3	VO : turn right

K

(seun-yuhng) kāat (信用)卡	6	N : credit card
kāat-pín 卡片	5	N : name card; business card
kàhm-máahn 琴晚	9/11	TW : last night
kàhm-yaht 琴日	4	TW : yesterday
káhn 近	14	ADJ : close to
kéuih 佢	5	PN : he; she; it
kéuih-deih 佢哋	5	PN : they
kìng 傾	15	V : to chat; to discuss

L

| lā 啦 | 6 | FP : let's; place |
| la 喇 | 9 | FP : already; indicating changes |

làahm-sīk 藍色	6	N :	blue
laaht 辣	16	ADJ :	hot and spicy
làih 嚟	9	V :	come
láih-baai-luhk 禮拜六	4	TW :	Saturday
láih-baai-ńgh 禮拜五	4	TW :	Friday
láih-baai-sàam 禮拜三	4	TW :	Wednesday
láih-baai-sei 禮拜四	4	TW :	Thursday
láih-baai-yaht 禮拜日	4	TW :	Sunday
láih-baai-yāt 禮拜一	4	TW :	Monday
láih-baai-yih 禮拜二	4	TW :	Tuesday
láu 樓	12	N :	floor
leng 靚	6	ADJ :	beautiful
léuih-hàhng 旅行	13	N :	travel; picnic; trip
līng-jáu 拎走	7	PH :	take away
lìhng-mūng chàh 檸檬茶	7	N :	lemon tea
lohk-yúh 落雨	13	VO :	rain
luhk 六	1	NU :	six
luhk-yuht 六月	4	N :	June
luhk-sīk 綠色	6	N :	green

M

maahn 萬	10	NU :	ten thousand
máaih 買	10	V :	buy
maaih 賣	12	V :	sell
màaih dāan 埋單	10	VO :	check the bill
máaih-yéh 買嘢	10	VO :	buy things; shopping
mahn 問	11	V :	to ask a question
mān 蚊	6	N :	dollar

māt-yéh 乜嘢	3/6	QW :	what; what kind of
māt-yéh sīk 乜嘢色	6	QW :	what colour
mē 咩	10/15	FP :	mood of surprise; what
meih 未	16	P :	not yet
Méih-gwok 美國	15	PW :	United States
Méih-sàm Jáu-làuh 美心酒樓	12	PW :	Maxim's Restaurant
m̀h 唔	5	P :	not
m̀h-gei-dāk 唔記得	13	V :	forget
m̀h-gòi 唔該	2	PH :	thank you; excuse me; please
m̀h-hōu-yi-sì 唔好意思	2	PH :	sorry
m̀h-sái 唔使	2/11	PH :	no need to
m̀h-syù-fuhk 唔舒服	13	ADJ/N :	uncomfortable, sick
mòhng 忙	9	ADJ :	busy
móuh 冇	6	V :	do not have
móuh mahn-tàih 冇問題	2	PH :	no problem, no worries
mùhn-háu 門口	3/12	N :	entrance; doorway

N

náaih-chàh 奶茶	7	N :	milk tea
nàahm 難	15	ADJ :	difficult
nám 諗	15	V :	think
néih 你	5	PN :	you
néih-deih 你哋	5	PN :	you (plural)
Néih hóu 你好	2	PH :	Nice to meet you
Néih hóu ma? 你好嗎？	5	PH :	How are you?
ńgh 五	1	NU :	five
ńgh-yuht 五月	4	N :	May

ngāam 啱	12	ADJ :	correct
ngàhn-hòhng 銀行 (M: gàan 間)	14	N :	bank
ngàhn-sīk 銀色	6	N :	silver
ngóh 我	5	PN :	I; me
ngóh-deih 我哋	5	PN :	we
Ngóh dōu haih 我都係	10	PH :	Me too
nī 呢	5	SP :	this
nī-douh 呢度	3	PW :	here
nī-go láih-baai 呢個禮拜	13	TW :	this week
nī-go sīng-kèih 呢個星期	13	TW :	this week
nī-go yuht 呢個月	13	TW :	this month
nìhn 年	15	TW :	year
noih 耐	15	ADJ :	long time

P

pàhng-yáuh 朋友	5	N :	friend
pèhng 平	6	ADJ :	cheap
pìhng-sìh 平時	15	TW :	usually; normally
pou-táu 舖頭 (M: gàan 間)	14	N :	shop

S

sā-téut 沙律	7	N :	salad
sāam 衫 (M: gihn 件)	6	N :	clothes
sàam 三	1	NU :	three
sàam-màhn-jih 三文治	7	N :	sandwich
sàam-yuht 三月	4	N :	March
Sāan-déng 山頂	16	PW :	The Peak
sàang-bé 生啤	11	N :	draft beer

sàang-yaht 生日	12	N :	birthday
sahp 十	1	NU :	ten
sahp-yāt-yuht 十一月	4	N :	November
sahp-yih-yuht 十二月	4	N :	December
sahp-yuht 十月	4	N :	October
sai 細	6	ADJ :	small
sāi-gwā 西瓜	7	N :	water melon
sái-sáu-gāan 洗手間 (M: go 個)	14	PW :	toilet
Saì-gung 西貢	16	PW :	Sai Kung
Sàm-jan 深圳	15	PW :	Shenzhen
sàn 新	6	ADJ :	new
Sàn Sai-gaai Daaih-hah 新世界大廈	14	PW :	New World Tower
sāp 濕	13	ADJ :	wet ; humid
sàu-gùng 收工	12	VO :	finish work
sei 四	1	NU :	four
sei-yuht 四月	4	N :	April
seuhng-go láih-baai 上個禮拜	13	TW :	last week
seuhng-go sīng-kèih 上個星期	13	TW :	last week
seuhng-go yuht 上個月	13	TW :	last month
seuhng-bihn 上便	14	PW :	above; on top of
seuhng-mihn 上面	14	PW :	above; on top of
seuhng-nín 上年	15	TW :	last year
séuhng-tòhng 上堂	8	VO :	attend a class
séui 水	10	N :	water
séung 想	10	AV :	want to; wish to
si-hah 試吓	6	VO :	try
sih-dō-bē-léi 士多啤梨	7	N :	strawberry
sìh-sìh 時時	12/13	ADV :	very often; always

sīk 識	3/14	V :	know how to ; have knowledge of; to know (somebody)
sihk 食	8	V :	eat
sihk aan 食晏	9/11	VO :	eat lunch
sihk faahn 食飯	7	VO :	have a meal
sihk jóu-chāan 食早餐	9	VO :	eat breakfast
sihk máahn-faahn 食晚飯	9	VO :	eat dinner
sìn 先	16	ADV :	first
sìn-sàang 先生	5	N :	Mr; husband; teacher
sing 姓	10	N :	surname
sīng-kèih-luhk 星期六	4	TW :	Saturday
sīng-kèih-ńgh 星期五	4	TW :	Friday
sīng-kèih-sàam 星期三	4	TW :	Wednesday
sīng-kèih-sei 星期四	4	TW :	Thursday
sīng-kèih-yaht 星期日	4	TW :	Sunday
sīng-kèih-yāt 星期一	4	TW :	Monday
sīng-kèih-yih 星期二	4	TW :	Tuesday
síu-bā 小巴 (M: ga 架)	3	N :	minibus
síu-jé 小姐	5	N :	Miss; young lady
síu-síu 少少	14	ADJ :	a little
syù 書 (M: bún 本)	11	N :	book
syù-fuhk 舒服	13	ADJ :	comfortable
syùn 酸	16	ADJ :	sour
syùhn 船 (M: jek 隻)	3	N :	ferry; boat

T

Taai-gwok choi 泰國菜	16	N :	Thai cuisine

taai-táai 太太	5	N :	Mrs; wife; lady (married)
tái dihn-sih 睇電視	9	VO :	watch television
tái syù 睇書	11	VO :	read a book
tái-háh 睇吓	6	PH :	take a look; depend on
tái hei 睇戲	9	VO :	see movie
tèng 聽	16	V :	listen; hear
tìhm 甜	16	ADJ :	sweet
tìhm-bán 甜品	11	N :	dessert
tìhng 停	3	V :	stop
tìn-hei 天氣	13	N :	weather
tīng-máahn 聽晚	16	TW :	tomorrow night
tīng-yaht 聽日	4	TW :	tomorrow
tói 枱 (M: jèung 張)	11	N :	table
tòng 湯	11	N :	soup
tóuh-ngoh 肚餓	9	ADJ :	hungry
tùhng 同	9	CON :	and; together with
Tùhng-lòh-wāan 銅鑼灣	12	PW :	Causeway Bay
tùhng-sih 同事	5	N :	colleague

U

ūk-kéi 屋企	8	N :	home
ūk-kéi-yàhn 屋企人	15/16	N :	family

W

waahk-jé 或者	13	ADV :	may be
wáan 玩	15/16	V :	have fun; play
Wāan-jái 灣仔	3	PW :	Wan Chai
wah 話	10	V :	to say

wàhn-tàn mihn 雲吞麵	9	N :	wonton with noodles
wo 喎	12	FP :	implies telling new situation; to remind
Wohng-gok 旺角	16	PW :	Mong Kok
wòhng-sīk 黃色	6	N :	yellow
wúih 會	15	AV :	will probably, will
wún 碗 (M: jek 隻 / go 個)	7/11	N :	bowl

Y

yàhn 人 (M: go 個)	11	N :	people
yaht 日	15	TW :	day
Yaht-bún choi 日本菜	16	N :	Japanese cuisine
yaht yaht 日日	12	PH :	everyday
yám 飲	7	V :	drink
yám-būi 飲杯	11	VO :	Cheers!; have a drink
yám-chàh 飲茶	10	VO :	drink tea; have tea and dim sum
yàm-tìn 陰天	13	N :	cloudy
yàn-waih 因為	9	CON :	because
yāt 一	1	NU :	one
yāt-chàih 一齊	9	ADV :	together
yāt-jahn 一陣	15	TW :	a moment
yāt-yuht 一月	4	N :	January
yáuh 有	6	V :	possess; have; exist
yauh-bihn 右便	14	PW :	right side
yáuh-lohk 有落	3	PH :	stop
yauh-mihn 右面	14	PW :	right side

yáuh-sìh 有時	10/13	ADV :	sometimes
yeh-máahn 夜晚	12	TW :	in the evening; night
Yi-daaih-leih choi 意大利菜	16	N :	Italian cuisine
yih 二	1	NU :	two
yih-yuht 二月	4	N :	February
yìh-gā 而家	4	TW :	now
yìhn-hauh 然後	9	CON :	and then, afterwards
yíng-séung 影相	11	VO :	take a photo
yiht 熱	7	ADJ :	hot
Yīng-gwok 英國	5	N :	United Kingdom
Yīng-màhn 英文	11/14	N :	English
yiu 要	7/11	V/AV :	want; need
yú 魚 (M: tìuh 條)	11	N :	fish
yùh-gwó 如果	14	CON :	if
yuht 月	4	TW :	month
Yuht-nàahm choi 越南菜	16	N :	Vietnamese cuisine

Appendix 2

English to Cantonese

A

a little	síu-síu 少少
a lot	hóu dò 好多
above	seuhng-mihn 上面 / seuhng-bihn 上便
Admiralty	Gām-jūng 金鐘
afterwards	jì-hauh 之後, yìhn-hauh 然後
airplane	fēi-gēi 飛機 (M: ga 架)
allow to	dāk 得
also	dōu 都
always	sìh-sìh 時時
and	tùhng 同
and then	yìhn-hauh 然後
April	sei-yuht 四月
arrive	dou 到
ask	mahn 問 (question)
assist	bōng 幫
at	hái 喺
at the traffic light	dāng-wái 燈位

attend a class	séuhng-tòhng 上堂
August	baat-yuht 八月

B

back	hauh-mihn 後面 / hauh-bihn 後便
bad	chā 差
bag	dói 袋 (M: go 個)
bank	ngàhn-hòhng 銀行 (M: gàan 間)
BBQ pork bun	chà-sìu-bāau 叉燒包
BBQ pork with rice	chà-sìu faahn 叉燒飯
beautiful	leng 靚
because	yàn-waih 因為
beer	bē-jáu 啤酒
before	jì-chìhn 之前
begin	hòi-chì 開始
below	hah-mihn 下面 / hah-bihn 下便
big	daaih 大
bill	dāan 單 (M: jèung 張)
birthday	sàang-yaht 生日
bitter	fú 苦
black	hāak-sīk 黑色
blue	làahm-sīk 藍色
boat	syùhn 船 (M: jek 隻)
boiling water	gwán séui 滾水
book	syù 書 (M: bún 本)
doorway	mùhn-háu 門口
bowl	wún 碗 (M: jek 隻 / go 個)

box	hahp 盒
brown	(ga-)fē-sīk（咖）啡色
bus	bā-sí 巴士 (M: ga 架)
business card	kāat-pín 卡片 (M: go 個/jèung 張)
busy	mòhng 忙
but	daahn-haih 但係
buy	máaih 買
buy things	máaih-yéh 買嘢

C

can	dāk 得, gwun 罐 (measure)
Cantonese	Gwóng-dùng-wá 廣東話
Causeway Bay	Tùhng-lòh-wāan 銅鑼灣
Central	Jùng-wàahn 中環
chat	kìng 傾
cheap	pèhng 平
Cheers!	yám-būi 飲杯
Chinese cuisine	Jùng-gwok choi 中國菜
Chinese	Jùng-màhn 中文
Chiuchow cuisine	Chīuh-jāu choi 潮州菜
chopsticks	faai-jí 筷子 (M: deui 對/sèung 雙)
close to	káhn 近
clothes	sāam 衫 (M: gihn 件)
cloudy	yàm-tìn 陰天
coffee	ga-fē 咖啡
coke	hó-lohk 可樂
cold	dung 凍

cold water	dung séui 凍水
colleague	tùhng-sih 同事
come	làih 嚟
comfortable	syù-fuhk 舒服
company	gūng-sī 公司 (M: gàan 間)
convenient	fòng-bihn 方便
correct	ngāam 啱
cost how much	géi(-dō) chín 幾(多)錢
credit card	(seun-yuhng) kāat (信用)卡
cup	būi 杯 (M: jek 隻/go 個)

D

day	yaht 日
day (of a month)	houh 號
December	sahp-yih-yuht 十二月
degree	douh 度
delicious	hóu-sihk 好食
dessert	tìhm-bán 甜品
difficult	nàahm 難
dim sum	dím-sām 點心
discount	jit 折
discuss	kìng 傾
do	jouh 做
dollar	mān 蚊
draft beer	sàang-bē 生啤
drink	yám 飲
drink tea	yám-chàh 飲茶
drive	jà-chè 揸車

E

eat	sihk 食 / sihk faahn 食飯
eat breakfast	sihk jóu-chāan 食早餐
eat dinner	sihk máahn-faahn 食晚飯
eat here	hái douh sihk 喺度食
eat lunch	sihk aan(-jau faahn) 食晏（晝飯）
egg	dáan 蛋 (M: jek 隻)
eight	baat 八
English	Yīng-màhn 英文
enjoy	wáan 玩
entrance	mùhn-háu 門口 (M: go 個)
equal to	haih 係
everyday	yaht yaht 日日 / múih-yaht 每日
excuse me	m̀h-gòi 唔該; m̀h-hóu-yi-sì 唔好意思
expensive	gwai 貴

F

family	ūk-kéi-yàhn 屋企人
faster	faai-dī 快啲
February	yih-yuht 二月
ferry	syùhn 船 (M: jek 隻)
fine	hóu 好
fine weather	hóu-tìn 好天
finish work	sàu-gùng 收工
first	sìn 先
fish	yú 魚 (M: tìuh 條)
five	ńgh or ḿh 五
floor	láu 樓

forget   m̀h-gei-dāk 唔記得

four   sei 四

French cuisine   Faat-gwok choi 法國菜

Friday   sīng-kèih-ńgh 星期五/láih-baai-ńgh 禮拜五

friend   pàhng-yáuh 朋友

front   chìhn-mihn 前面/chìhn-bihn 前便

full (stomach)   báau 飽

G

get up   héi-sàn 起身

give   béi 畀

glass   būi 杯 (M: jek 隻 /go 個)

go   heui 去

go out   chēut heui 出去

go home   fàan ūk-kéi 返屋企

go straight   jihk heui 直去

gold   gām-sīk 金色 (colour)

good   hóu 好

Good morning   jóu-sàhn 早晨

goodbye   bāai-baai 拜拜

green   luhk-sīk 綠色

grey   fùi-sīk 灰色

ground   deih-há 地下

H

happy   hòi-sàm 開心

ham   fó-téui 火腿

have	yáuh 有
have a drink	yám-būi 飲杯
have a meal	sihk faahn 食飯
have free (time)	dāk-hàahn 得閒
have fun	wáan 玩
have not	móuh 冇
have tea & dim sum	yám-chàh 飲茶
Haven't seen you for a long time	Hóu noih móuh gin 好耐冇見
he	kéuih 佢
hear	tèng 聽
help	bōng 幫
here	nī-douh 呢度
(have a) holiday	fong-ga 放假
home	ūk-kéi 屋企
Hong Kong	Hèung-góng 香港
hope	hēi-mohng 希望
hot	yiht 熱
hotel	jáu-dim 酒店 (M: gàan 間)
hour	jùng-tàuh 鐘頭
how	dím-yéung 點樣
How are you?	Néih hóu ma? 你好嗎？
how long	géi-noih or géi-loih 幾耐 (time)
how many	géi-dō 幾多
hundred	baak 百
hungry	tóuh-ngoh 肚餓
husband	sìn-sàang 先生

I

I	ngóh 我
ice water	bīng-seui 冰水
if	yùh-gwó 如果
in	hái 喺
in the evening	yeh-máahn 夜晚
interesting	hóu-tái 好睇 (see or read); hóu-wáan 好玩 (have fun)
invite	chéng 請
It is true	haih a 係呀
Italian cuisine	Yi-daaih-leih choi 意大利菜

J

January	yāt-yuht 一月
Japanese cuisine	Yaht-bún choi 日本菜
July	chāt-yuht 七月
June	luhk-yuht 六月

K

know	jì 知 (facts); sīk 識 (knowledge; people)
Korean cuisine	Hòhn-gwok choi 韓國菜
Kowloon	Gáu-lùhng 九龍

L

lady	taai-táai 太太 (married)
large	daaih 大
last month	seuhng-go yuht 上個月
last night	kàhm-máahn 琴晚

last week	seuhng-go sīng-kèih 上個星期/ seuhng-go láih-baai 上個禮拜
last year	gauh-nín 舊年/seuhng-nín 上年
later on	jì-hauh 之後
learn	hohk 學
leave	jáu 走
left side	jó-mihn 左面/jó-bihn 左便
lemon tea	lìhng-mūng-chàh 檸檬茶
like	jùng-yi 鍾意
listen	tèng 聽
live	jyuh 住
located at	hái 喺

M

many	hóu dò 好多; dò 多
March	sàam-yuht 三月
market	gàai-síh 街市 (M: go 個)
May	ńgh-yuht 五月
may be	waahk-jé 或者
may I ask?	chéng-mahn 請問
me	ngóh 我
me too	ngóh dōu haih 我都係
meet	gin 見
(have a) meeting	hòi-wúi 開會
milk tea	náaih-chàh 奶茶
minibus	síu-bā 小巴
minute	fàn-jùng 分鐘 (time spent); fàn 分
Miss	síu-jé 小姐

Misses	taai-táai 太太
Mister	sìn-sàang 先生
Monday	sīng-kèih-yāt 星期一 / láih-baai-yāt 禮拜一
money	chín 錢
Mong Kok	Wohng-gok 旺角
month	yuht 月
more	dò-dī 多啲; ADJ + dī 啲
most	jeui 最
movie	hei 戲 (M: tou 套); tái hei 睇戲 (see a movie)
MTR	deih-tit 地鐵
MTR station	deih-tit jaahm 地鐵站 (M: go 個)
much	dò 多
mug	būi 杯

N

name card	kāat-pín 卡片
National Day	Gwok-hing 國慶
near	káhn 近
nearby	fuh-gahn 附近
need	yiu 要
new	sàn 新
next month	hah-go yuht 下個月
next week	hah-go sīng-kèi 下個星期 / hah-go láih-baai 下個禮拜
next year	chēut-nín 出年 / hah-nín 下年
Nice to meet you	Néih hóu 你好
night	yeh-máahn 夜晚
nine	gáu 九
no need to	m̀h-sái 唔使

no problem	móuh mahn-tàih 冇問題
normally	pìhng-sìh 平時
not	m̀h 唔
not here	m̀h-hái-douh 唔喺度
not yet	meih 未
November	sapt-yāt yuht 十一月
now	yìh-gā 而家
number	houh 號

O

o'clock	dím 點
October	sapt-yuht 十月
office	gūng-sī 公司
okay	dāk 得
on top of	seuhng-mihn 上面/seuhng-bihn 上便
one	yāt 一
oneself	jih-géi 自己
opposite side	deui-mihn 對面
or	dihng (-haih) 定(係)
orange	cháang 橙, cháang-sīk 橙色 (colour)

P

people	yàhn 人 (M: go 個)
picnic	léuih-hàhng 旅行
pink	fán-hùhng-sīk 粉紅色
play	wáan 玩
please	m̀h-gòi 唔該
plenty	hóu dò 好多; dò 多

poor   chā 差 (poor skill); móuh chín 冇錢 (no money)

possess   yáuh 有

prawn   hā 蝦

purple   jí-sīk 紫色

Q

quick   faai 快; faai-dī 快啲 (quickly, faster)

quite   géi 幾 ＋ ADJ

R

rain   lohk-yúh 落雨

rarely   hóu síu 好少

really   jàn-haih 真係

receipt   dāan 單 (M: jèung 張)

recently   jeui-gahn 最近

red   hùhng-sīk 紅色

remember   gei-dāk 記得

reserve table   dehng tói 訂枱 (table)

restaurant   chāan-tēng 餐廳 (M: gàan 間)
  jáu-làuh 酒樓 (Chinese restaurant)

rice   faahn 飯

right side   yauh-mihn 右面／yauh-bihn 右便

run   jáu 走

S

Sai Kung   Saì-gung 西貢

salad   sā-léut 沙律

salty   hàahm 鹹

sandwich	sàam-màhn-jih 三文治
Saturday	sīng-kèih-luhk 星期六/làih-baai-luhk 禮拜六
seafood	hói-sìn 海鮮
see you	joi-gin 再見
seldom	hóu síu 好少
sell	maaih 賣
September	gáu-yuht 九月
serving chopsticks	gūng-faai 公筷 (M: deui 對)
seven	chāt 七
she	kéuih 佢
shoes	hàaih 鞋 (M: deui 對)
shop	pou-táu 舖頭 (M: gàan 間)
shopping	máaih-yéh 買嘢
shrimp	hā 蝦
sick	m̀h-syù-fuhk 唔舒服
silver	ngàhn-sīk 銀色 (colour)
six	luhk 六
sleep	fan-gaau 瞓覺
small	sai 細
sometimes	yáuh-sìh 有時
sorry	m̀h-hóu-yi-sì 唔好意思/deui-m̀h-jyuh 對唔住
soup	tòng 湯
sour	syùn 酸
speak	góng 講
spicy	laaht 辣
stop	tìhng 停; yáuh lohk 有落
strawberry	sih-dō-bē-léi 士多啤梨

street conrner	gàai-háu 街口 (M: go 個)
Sunday	sīng-kèih-yaht 星期日／láih-baai-yaht 禮拜日
surname	sing 姓
sweet	tìhm 甜

T

table	tói 枱 (M: jèung 張)
take a photo	yíng-séung 影相
take a transport	daap-chè 搭車
take away	līng-jáu 拎走
taxi	dīk-sí 的士 (M: ga 架)
tea	chàh 茶
teach	gaau 教
teacher	sìn-sàang 先生
telephone	dihn-wá 電話 (M: go 個)
ten	sahp 十
ten cents	houh-jí 毫子
ten thousand	maahn 萬
Thai cuisine	Taai-gwok choi 泰國菜
thank you	m̀h-gòi 唔該；dò-jeh 多謝 (for gifts or meals, congratulations, invitations, appreciation)
that	gó 嗰 ＋ M
The Peak	Sāan-déng 山頂
then	jauh 就；jì-hauh 之後；yìhn-hauh 然後
there	gó-douh 嗰度
they	kéuih-deih 佢哋
thing	yéh 嘢

this	nī 呢 + M
this month	gàm-go yuht 今個月 / nī-go yuht 呢個月
this week	gàm-go sīng-kèih 今個星期 / gàm-go láih-baai 今個禮拜 nī-go sīng-kèih 呢個星期 / nī-go láih-baai 呢個禮拜
this year	gàm-nín or gàm-nìhn 今年
thousand	chìn 千
three	sàam 三
Thursday	sīng-kèih-sei 星期四 / láih-baai-sei 禮拜四
times	chi 次
tired	gwuih 劫
to	dou 到
to say	wah 話
today	gàm-yaht 今日
together with	tùhng 同
toilet	sái-sáu-gāan 洗手間 / chi-só 廁所 (M: go 個)
tomorrow	tīng-yaht 聽日
tomorrow night	tīng-máahn 聽晚
tram	dihn-chè 電車 (M: ga 架)
travel	léuih-hàhng 旅行 (M: chi 次)
treat	chéng 請
trip	léuih-hàhng 旅行 (M: chi 次)
try	si-hah 試吓
Tsim Sha Tsui	Jìm-sà-jćui 尖沙咀
Tuesday	sīng-kèih-yih 星期二 / láih-baai-yih 禮拜二
turn left	jyun jó 轉左
turn right	jyun yauh 轉右
two	yih 二; léuhng 兩 + M
typhoon	dá-fùng 打風

U

uncomfortable	m̀h-syù-fuhk 唔舒服
under	hah-mihn 下面/hah-bihn 下便
United Kingdom	Yīng-gwok 英國
until	ji 至
U.S.A.	Méih-gwok 美國
usually	pìhng-sìh 平時

V

vegetables	choi 菜
very	hóu 好
very often	sìh-sìh 時時
Vietnamese cuisine	Yuht-nàahm choi 越南菜

W

wait	dáng (dáng) 等（等）
walk	hàahng-louh 行路
Wan Chai	Wāan-jái 灣仔
want	yiu 要/séung yiu 想要
want to	séung 想
watch TV	tái dihn-sih 睇電視
water	séui 水
water melon	sāi-gwā 西瓜 (M: go 個)
we	ngóh-deih 我哋
weather	tìn-hei 天氣
Wednesday	sīng-kèih-sāam 星期三/láih-baai-sāam 禮拜三
welcome	fun-yìhng gwòng làhm 歡迎光臨
well	gám 咁

wet	sāp 濕
what	māt-yéh 乜嘢; mē 咩
what colour	māt-yéh sīk 乜嘢色
what date	géi(-dō)-houh 幾(多)號
what time	géi(-dō)-dím 幾(多)點
when	géi-sìh 幾時
where	bīn-douh 邊度
which floor	géi(-dō) láu 幾(多)樓
which month	bīn-go yuht 邊個月 / géi(-dō)-yuht 幾(多)月
which of these	bīn-dī 邊啲
which side	bīn-mihn 邊面 / bīn-bihn 邊便
white	baahk-sīk 白色
who	bīn-go 邊個
why	dím-gáai 點解
wife	taai-táai 太太
will	wúih 會
wish	héi-mohng 希望
wish to	séung 想
wonton with noodles	wàhn-tàn mihn 雲吞麵
work	fàan-gùng 返工 (go to work); jouh-yéh 做嘢

Y

year	nìhn 年
yellow	wòhng-sīk 黃色
yesterday	kàhm-yaht 琴日
you	néih 你; néih-deih 你哋 (plural)
young lady	síu-jé 小姐

Appendix 3

Cantonese slang

(Track 196)

a-jē 阿姐	a very competent lady, a way to address cleaner and tea lady
AA jai A A 制	share the bill, go Dutch
àau-saai tàuh 揪晒頭	completely lost (in an idea) (lit: scratch one's head)
baahn-yéh 扮嘢	pretend to be important
báai wù-lúng 擺烏龍	make a mistake
baat-gwa 八卦	nosy
bāau-mēi or bāau-méih 包尾	at the end of the list
baih lak 弊嘞	That's too bad
béi-háh mín 畀吓面	give me some face
bok-mehng 搏命	work desperately (lit: risk life)
bok-yāt-bok 搏一搏	try one's luck
bun-túng-séui 半桶水	having only a little knowledge (lit: half bucket of water)

(Track 197)

chaat-hàaih-jái 擦鞋仔	a 'yes' man (lit: shoe-shine boy)

cháau gú-piu 炒股票	to speculate on stocks and shares
cháau láu 炒樓	to speculate on real estate properties
cháau yàuh-yú 炒魷魚	to dismiss someone (from his job) (lit: stir-fry squid)
chèuhng-hei 長氣	long-winded
chéun-gwo jek jyù 蠢過隻豬	more stupid than a pig
chēut-wái 出位	doing what one should not do; outstanding
chì-sin 黐線	crazy (lit: wires crossed)
chói néih dōu sòh 睬你都傻	I won't bother about you
chòu-lóuh 粗魯	rude

(Track 198)

dá-dāk síu 打得少	deserve beating up
dá-gēi 打機	to play computer games
dá-jìm 打尖	to jump queue
dá syù-sou 打輸數	prepare for the worst
dá-wàahng-làih góng 打橫嚟講	being unreasonable (lit: talk horizontally)
daaih-lóu 大佬	big brother; a leader of a gang
daaih-saai 大晒	appearing to be the most authoritative
daaih-tàuh-hā 大頭蝦	absent-minded (lit: a big headed prawn)
daaih-yi 大意	careless
daaih-yíh-lūng 大耳窿	a loanshark (lit: big ear hole)
daap-tói 搭枱	to share a table
dái-séi 抵死	ask for it (lit: deserve death)
dái-sek 抵錫	deserving favour
dāk ga la 得㗎喇	That's OK.; That's good enough

dihng-dī làih 定啲嚟	keep calm; be calm
dím-syun hóu 點算好？	what can be done?
díng-m̀h-seuhn 頂唔順	cannot put up with
dohng-sāt louh 蕩失路	get lost on the way
dūk bui-jek 篤背脊	backstab

(Track 199)

fáan-mín 反面	become enemies, suddenly turn hostile (lit: turn over face)
faat-daaht 發達	lucky, make a fortune
faat ngauh-dauh 發吽豆	look dull or bored
faat pèih-hei 發脾氣	lose one's temper
fong fèi-gèi 放飛機	stood somebody up
fong gwo ngóh 放過我	leave me alone; give me a break
fut-lóu 濶佬	generous

(Track 200)

gáau bīn-fō a? 搞邊科呀？	What are you trying to do?
gáau cho a! 搞錯呀！	It's a mistake!
gáau-dihm 搞掂	It's done!
gáau-gáau-jan 搞搞震	goofing around
gáau-siu 搞笑	hilarious
gáu-m̀h-daap-baat 九唔搭八	be unrelated, nonsense
gihng 勁	powerful
gīk-hei 激氣	irritated; annoyed
gīk-séi-yàhn 激死人	very irritating; very annoying
gwàan léih mē sih 關你咩事	none of your business

gwai dou fèi-héi 貴到飛起	outrageously expensive
gwū-hòhn 孤寒	mean, misery
gú-waahk-jái 古惑仔	mafia; gangster

(Track 201)

hāak(-jái) 黑（仔）	have bad luck (lit: black boy)
hāan chín 慳錢	save money
háu-sò 口疏	not able to keep secrets (lit: mouth sparse)
hèung(-jó) 香（咗）	to be dead; It's a failure
hóu gwo móuh 好過冇	better than nothing

(Track 202)

jà-fīt 揸弗	be in charge
jāp-lāp 執笠	to close down (a shop or company)
jáu-bóu 走寶	miss a good chance
jáu-gāi 走雞	miss a chance (lit: run away a chicken)
jeng 正	excellent
jeuhk-sou 着數	advantageous
jíng-gú 整蠱	to play a trick on someone
jok daaih 作大	embellish; boast; exaggerate
jyù-pá 豬扒	pork chop, ugly woman
jyù-pàhng-gáu-yáuh 豬朋狗友	friends with bad habits (lit: pig friends dog pals)
jyù-tàuh-bíng 豬頭丙	fool; blockhead

(Track 203)

kùhng-gwái 窮鬼	a very poor person
lá-yìhng 嫲型	a very efferminate man

làahm-yàhn-pòh 男人婆	a tomboy
laahp-saap 垃圾	rubbish; trash
lahp-láp-lyuhn 立立亂	in disorder
lauh-hei 漏氣	slow in action or decision making
léih góng yéh àh? 你講嘢吖？	Are you talking nonsense?
lèih-póu 離譜	illogical; unreasonable
Léih wah sih 你話事	You make the decision; It's all up to you
lēng-jái 靚仔	young boy
lēng-mūi 靚妹	young girl
leuhn-jeuhn 論盡	clumsy
lēuk-séui 掠水	to squeeze money from people; to tap water
lóuh-béng 老餅	old fashioned
lóuh-dím 老點	make a fool of somebody
lóuh-fúng 老奉	take things for granted
lóuh-tóu 老土	old-fashioned
lyún-làih 亂嚟	do things irresponsibly

(Track 204)

máih chòuh 咪嘈	shut up
m̀h-chì-gà 唔黐家	never at home (lit: not stuck home)
m̀h-deui-louh 唔對路	it doesn't look right
m̀h-gok-yi 唔覺意	unintentionally
m̀h-jì góng māt 唔知講乜	don't know what to say/don't know what he's talking about
m̀h-sái séi 唔使死	it doesn't cost your life
móuh gam hóu hei 冇咁好氣	would not give any attention to it

móuh léih fán 冇你份	you are not included
mòuh-lèih-tàuh 無厘頭	expressions or actions that mean nothing
móuh líu 冇料	not knowledgeable
móuh mín 冇面	lose face
móuh ngáahn tái 冇眼睇	hate to see it, pathetic (lit: no eye see)
móuh lóuh 冇腦	brainless
móuh sàm-gèi 冇心機	feeling melancholy
móuh yáhn 冇癮	weary; lack of interest
móuh yi-gin 冇意見	no comment
mùhng-chàh-chàh 朦查查	in a muddle vision

(Track 205)

ngāam-kì 啱key	to get along well (with people) (lit: the right key or tone in music)
ngohng-gèui 戇居	indifferent to hints, stupid
sàai hei 嘥氣	waste of effort
sài-leih 犀利	extreme good or bad
sám-jiu 心照	understand without the need for words (lit: heart shine)
sám-lèuhng 心涼	feel avenged (lit: heart cool)
sám-táahm 心淡	losing hope (lit: heart indifferent)
sāp-sāp-seui 濕濕碎	miscellaneous; trivial
sāt-wàhn-yú 失魂魚	an absent-minded person (lit: lost soul fish)
sàu sèng 收聲	shut up
sèh-wòhng 蛇王	to sneak away (lit: snake king)
sek-saai léih 錫晒你	you're my favourite, I love you so much

sèui dou séi 衰到死	you're so bad
séui-fo 水貨	imported goods without an agent ('parallel' imports)
sèui-jó 衰咗	to have failed
sih-daahn 是但	do as you like; whatever
sihk gūk-júng 食穀種	living on one's savings (lit: eat grain seeds)
sihk séi-māau 食死貓	falsely accused (lit: eat a dead cat)
siht-dái 蝕底	to lose out
sīk jouh 識做	know what is the smart thing to do
sīk taan 識嘆	know how to enjoy life
síng-muhk 醒目	smart
síu-hei 小器	narrow-minded
sìu-yé 宵夜	midnight snack
sòh gàh néih? 傻㗎你？	Are you crazy?; Are you nuts?
sòh-lóu 傻佬	a fool; an idot

(Track 206)

tái-síu 睇小	to belittle someone
tūng-déng 通頂	working overnight
wáan-yéh 玩嘢	provoke people
wáan-yùhn 玩完	game over
waht-daht 核突	disgusting, ugly
waih-sihk māau 為食貓	greedy; glutton
wán-bahn 搵笨	looking for a sucker
wū-jōu 污糟	dirty

(Track 207)

yài yài 曳曳	naughty (child)
yàm-sāp 陰濕	treachcrous
yāt-chi-gwo 一次過	all in one go
yáuh líu 有料	knowledgeable
Yáuh móuh gáau cho a? 有冇搞錯呀？	Have you made a mistake?; Are you for real?
yáuh-yìhng 有型	smart looking; cool
yéung-sèui 樣衰	bad looking (makes people dislike it)
yú dou baau 瘀到爆	very embarassing (lit: bruised to explosion)
yuhk-tung 肉痛	feel hurt when one lets something go (lit: flesh pain)

Suggested answers

LESSON 2

I.   *What do you say?*

1. Ṁh-gòi. 唔該。

2. jóu-sàhn. 早晨。

3. Ṁh-sái 唔使。

4. Faai-dī lā. 快啲啦。

5. Ṁh-gòi dáng dáng. 唔該等等。

6. Móuh mahn-tàih. 冇問題。

7. Ṁh-gòi. 唔該。

8. Bāai-baai. 拜拜。

9. Dò-jeh. 多謝。

10. Néih hóu. 你好。

11. Ṁh-hóu yi-sì. 唔好意思。

12. Haih a. 係呀。

II.   *Matching*

1. e   2. h   3. g   4. d   5. c   6. j   7. b   8. i   9. a   10. f

LESSON 4

Exercise I

1. Sahp-yih-yuht yah-ńgh houh, sīng-kèih-sei
   十 二 月 二 十 五 號 、 星 期 四

2. Chāt-yuht sàam-sahp houh, sīng-kèih-yāt
   七 月 三 十 號 、 星 期 一

3. Yih-yuht sei houh, sīng-kèih ńgh
二　月　四　號　、　星　期　五

4. Sei-yuht sahp-luhk houh, sīng-kèih-luhk
四　月　十　六　號　、　星　期　六

5. Sahp-yāt-yuht yih-sahp-chāt houh, sīng-kèih-sàam, léuhng dím
十　一　月　二　十　七　號　、　星　期　三　、　兩　點

6. Gáu-yuht sahp-yih houh, sīng-kèih-yaht, yāt dím gáu
九　月　十　二　號　、　星　期　日　、　一　點　九

7. Luhk-yuht gáu houh, sīng-kèih-yih, sahp dím bun
六　月　九　號　、　星　期　二　、　十　點　半

8. Ńgh-yuht baat houh, sīng-kèih-yāt, luhk dím ńgh
五　月　八　號　、　星　期　一　、　六　點　五

LESSON 5

B. Practice

1. a　　2. b　　3. c　　4. b　　5. a　　6. a　　7. c　　8. a

Review Exercise

I. Fill in the blanks

1. m̀h-haih 唔係

2. tùhng-sih 同事 /
   pàhng-yáuh 朋友

3. m̀h 唔

4. haih m̀h-haih...a 係唔係…呀

5. your name

II. Translation

1. Kéuih-deih haih m̀h-haih Hòh sìn-sàang ge tùhng-sih a?
   佢　哋　係　唔　係　何　先　生　嘅　同　事　呀　？

2. Kéuih haih m̀h-haih néih taai-táai a?
   佢　係　唔　係　你　太　太　呀　？

3. Chàhn síu-jé m̀h-haih Wòhng taai-táai ge pàhng-yáuh.

   陳 小 姐 唔 係 黃 太 太 嘅 朋 友 。

4. Kéuih haih kéuih-deih ge pàhng-yáuh, m̀h-haih ngóh tùhng-sih.

   佢 係 佢 哋 嘅 朋 友 ， 唔 係 我 同 事 。

5. Néih dihn-wá haih m̀h haih sàam luhk yih chāt ńgh luhk lìhng lìhng.

   你 電 話 係 唔 係 三 六 二 七 五 六 ○ ○ 。

6. M̀h-hóu-yi-sì, nī-go m̀h-haih Chàhn sìn-sàang ge kāat-pín.

   唔 好 意 思 ， 呢 個 唔 係 陳 先 生 嘅 咭 片 。

7. Néih haih bīn-wái / bīn-go a?

   你 係 邊 位 / 邊 個 呀 ？

8. Kéuih haih ngóh sìn-sàang.

   佢 係 我 先 生 。

Listening Exercise

I.

1. d   2. d   3. a   4. c

II. *(Track 062)*

1. Ji-mìhng haih Chàhn sìn-sàang ge taai-táai.   (F)

   志 明 係 陳 先 生 嘅 太 太 。

2. Hòh síu-jé haih Chàhn sàang ge pàhng-yáuh.   (F)

   何 小 姐 係 陳 生 嘅 朋 友 。

3. Chàhn sìn-sàang m̀h-haih Léih sìn-sàang ge tùhng-sih.   (T)

   陳 先 生 唔 係 李 先 生 嘅 同 事 。

4. Wòhng sàang haih Hòh síu-jé ge sìn-sàang.   (T)

   王 生 係 何 小 姐 嘅 先 生 。

5. Chàhn sàang m̀h-haih Léih táai pàhng-yáuh.   (T)

   陳 生 唔 係 李 太 朋 友 。

6. Ji-mìhng haih Hòh síu-jé ge tùhng-sih.   (F)

　志　明　係　何　小　姐　嘅　同　事　。

7. Léih sàang haih Wòhng sàang ge pàhng-yáuh.   (T)

　李　生　係　王　生　嘅　朋　友　。

LESSON 6

A. Money — Practice

II. Listen and write down the amount of money

1. $18.40	2. $0.60	3. $63.50	4. $21.90	5. $57.20
6. $4.10	7. $35.30	8. $0.20	9. $89.40	10. $92.60

Review Exercise — Translation

1. yáuh móuh làahm-sīk sāam a?

　有　冇　藍　色　衫　呀　？

2. Pèhng-dī lā. Ńgh-sahp-mān dāk lā.

　平　啲　啦　。　五　十　蚊　得　啦　。

3. Nī-go dói móuh cháang-sīk.

　呢　個　袋　冇　橙　色　。

4. Māt-yéh sīk a?

　乜　嘢　色　呀　？

5. Wòhng-sīk ge chāt-sahp-ńgh mān, hùhng-sīk ge sàam-sahp-baat mān.

　黃　色　嘅　七　十　五　蚊　，　紅　色　嘅　三　十　八　蚊　。

6. Fán-hùhng-sīk ge yáuh móuh daaih-dī ga?

　粉　紅　色　嘅　有　冇　大　啲　㗎　？

7. Bīn-go sàn-dī a?

　邊　個　新　啲　呀　？

Listening Exercise

I. *(Track 074)*

1. hùhng-sīk 紅色, green (N)
2. daaih-dī 大啲, bigger (Y)
3. fán-hùhng-sīk 粉紅色, pink (Y)
4. luhk jit 六折, 30% off (N)
5. $18.70, $16.70 (N)
6. sàn-dī 新啲, cheaper (N)

II. *(Track 075)*

1. Nī-yeuhng yéh (*this object) yáuh géi-dō jit a? (c)
   呢 樣 嘢 有 幾 多 折 呀 ?

2. Nī-yeuhng yéh géi-dō chín a? (d)
   呢 樣 嘢 幾 多 錢 呀 ?

3. Nī-yeuhng yéh géi-dō chín a? (b)
   呢 樣 嘢 幾 多 錢 呀 ?

4. Nī-yeuhng yéh yáuh géi-dō jit a? (a)
   呢 樣 嘢 有 幾 多 折 呀 ?

5. Nī-yeuhng yéh yáuh móuh wòhng-sīk a? (b)
   呢 樣 嘢 有 冇 黃 色 呀 ?

6. Nī-yeuhng yéh yáuh māt-yéh sīk a? (c)
   呢 樣 嘢 有 乜 嘢 色 呀 ?

LESSON 7

A. Practice

Translate and answer the questions

1. Néih daap dīk-sí dihng bā-sí a?
   你 搭 的 士 定 巴 士 呀 ?

2. Yiht dihng dung ga-fē a?
   熱 定 凍 咖 啡 呀 ？

3. Sih-dō-bē-léi dihng cháang a?
   士 多 啤 梨 定 橙 呀 ？

4. Yih-yuht dihng gáu-yuht a?
   二 月 定 九 月 呀 ？

5. Léuhng māan dihng yih-sahp māan a?
   兩 蚊 定 二 十 蚊 呀 ？

6. Sàam-dím dihng sàam-dím-bun a?
   三 點 定 三 點 半 呀 ？

7. Néih heui Jùng-wàahn dihng Wāan-jái a?
   你 去 中 環 定 灣 仔 呀 ？

8. Sahp wún dihng sahp-yih wún faahn a?
   十 碗 定 十 二 碗 飯 呀 ？

B. Practice

1. Ngóh béi baat-sahp-ńgh māan néih.
   我 畀 八 十 五 蚊 你 。

2. M̀h-gòi béi (néih) go dihn-wá ngóh.
   唔 該 畀 （ 你 ） 個 電 話 我 。

3. Néih pàhng-yáuh béi dī māt-yéh néih a?
   你 朋 友 畀 啲 乜 嘢 你 呀 ？

4. Ngóh béi nī-go baahk-sīk ge bīn-go a?
   我 畀 呢 個 白 色 嘅 邊 個 呀 ？

5. Bīn-go béi būi náaih-chàh ngóh a?
   邊 個 畀 杯 奶 茶 我 呀 ？

Review exercise

II. Translation

1. Ngóh yám dung ga-fē. 我 飲 凍 咖 啡 。

2. Ngóh m̀h-yiu faahn. 我 唔 要 飯 。

3. Daaih dihng sai hó-lohk a? 大 定 細 可 樂 呀 ?

4. Léuhng go sàam-màhn-jih chāt-sahp-yih-go-yih.
   兩 個 三 文 治 七 十 二 個 二 。

5. Néih yiu géi-dò go sā-léut a?
   你 要 幾 多 個 沙 律 呀 ?

6. M̀h-gòi béi būi dung lìhng-mūng-chàh kéuih lā.
   唔 該 畀 杯 凍 檸 檬 茶 佢 啦 。

7. Sàam go cháang géi chín a?
   三 個 橙 幾 錢 呀 ?

8. Ńgh būi yiht lìhng-mūng chàh luhk-sahp mān.
   五 杯 熱 檸 檬 茶 六 十 蚊 。

9. M̀h-gòi béi (néih) go kāat-pín ngóh.
   唔 該 畀 （你） 個 咭 片 我 。

10. Ngóh béi yih-sahp mān bīn-go a?
    我 畀 二 十 蚊 邊 個 呀 ?

LESSON 8

Review Exercise — Translation

1. Néih géi-dím fàan ūk-kéi a?
   你 幾 點 返 屋 企 呀 ?

2. Ngóh yāt-dím sihk faahn.
   我 一 點 食 飯 。

3. Néih tùhng-sih sàam-dím-bun jouh māt-yéh a?
   你 同 事 三 點 半 做 乜 嘢 呀 ?

4. Néih pàhng-yáuh géi-dím séuhng-tòhng a?
   你 朋 友 幾 點 上 堂 呀 ?

5. Kéuih sahp-yāt-dím-gáu fan-gaau.
   佢 十 一 點 九 瞓 覺 。

6. Kéuih-deih m̀h-chēut-heui.
   佢 哋 唔 出 去 。

Listening Exercises *(Track 092)*

1. Néih yāt-dím sihk faahn àh?   (Haih 係)
   你 一 點 食 飯 吖 ?

2. Néih géi-dím héi-sàn a?   (chāt-dím 7:00)
   你 幾 點 起 身 呀 ?

3. Néih gáu-dím fàan-gùng àh?   (Haih 係)
   你 九 點 返 工 吖 ?

4. Néih géi-dím fàan ūk-kéi a?   (chāt-dím-bun 7:30)
   你 幾 點 返 屋 企 呀 ?

5. Néih géi-dím séuhng-tòhng a?   (luhk-dím 6:00)
   你 幾 點 上 堂 呀 ?

6. Néih géi-dím fan-gaau a?   (sahp-yāt-dím 11:00)
   你 幾 點 瞓 覺 呀 ?

7. Néih daap m̀h-daap deih-tit a?   (Daap 搭)
   你 搭 唔 搭 地 鐵 呀 ?

8. Néih daap m̀h-daap dīk-sí a?   (M̀h-daap 唔搭)
   你 搭 唔 搭 的 士 呀 ?

LESSON 9

B. Practice

1. Néih tùhng bīn-go sihk faahn a?
   你 同 邊 個 食 飯 呀 ?

2. Néih tùhng Léih sàang géi-dím sihk faahn a?
   你 同 李 生 幾 點 食 飯 呀 ？

3. Néih tùhng pàhng-yáuh sīng-kèih-géi heui yám chàh a?
   你 同 朋 友 星 期 幾 去 飲 茶 呀 ？

4. Néih tùhng m̀h tùhng Wòhng síu-jé tái hei a?
   你 同 唔 同 黃 小 姐 睇 戲 呀 ？

5. Néih tùhng tùhng-sih jouh māt-yéh a?
   你 同 同 事 做 乜 嘢 呀 ？

6. Néih tùhng pàhng-yáuh heui bīn-douh a?
   你 同 朋 友 去 邊 度 呀 ？

Review Final Particles

1. la 喇, lā 啦   2. àh 吖   3. lā 啦   4. a 呀 or ga 㗎

5. a 呀   6. la 喇   7. lā 啦   8. ga 㗎

Review Exercise

I.   Rewrite sentences

1. Ngóh gàm-yaht daap dīk-sí fàan ūk-kéi.
   我 今 日 搭 的 士 返 屋 企 。

2. Kéuih-deih sīng-kèih-sei yāt-dím sihk faahn.
   佢 哋 星 期 四 一 點 食 飯 。

3. Kéuih m̀h-tùhng taai-táai chēut heui.
   佢 唔 同 太 太 出 去 。

4. Ngóh pàhng-yáuh hóu dāk-hàahn.
   我 朋 友 好 得 閒 。

II. *Fill in the blanks*

1. fàan-gùng 返工
2. sihk faahn 食飯
3. pàhng-yáuh 朋友
4. tùhng m̀h-tùhng 同唔同
5. tùhng 同, sihk faahn 食飯

III. *Translation*

1. Ngóh baat-dím-gáu daap bā-sí fàan-gùng.
   我 八 點 九 搭 巴 士 返 工 。

2. Kéuih-deih chāt-dím-sàam làih, yìhn-hauh sahp-dím-bun fàan ūk-kéi.
   佢 哋 七 點 三 嚟 ， 然 後 十 點 半 返 屋 企 。

3. Ngóh m̀h-tùhng taai-táai sihk faahn.
   我 唔 同 太 太 食 飯 。

4. Ngóh sīng-kèih-ńgh m̀h-mòhng.
   我 星 期 五 唔 忙 。

5. Kéuih hóu gwuih.
   佢 好 劫 。

6. Néih tùhng bīn-go sihk faahn a?
   你 同 邊 個 食 飯 呀 ？

7. Ngóh yìh-gā fàan ūk-kéi.
   我 而 家 返 屋 企 。

8. Sīng-kèih-tuhk ngóh tùhng pàhng-yáuh chēut heui.
   星 期 六 我 同 朋 友 出 去 。

Listening Exercise

I.

1. d   2. d   3. a   4. b

II. *(Track 104)*

1. Kéuih heui bīn-douh a?   (Jùng-wàahn fàan-gùng 中環返工)
   佢 去 邊 度 呀 ？

2. Kéuih daap géi-dō houh bā-sí a?   (sahp houh 10號)
   佢 搭 幾 多 號 巴 士 呀 ？

3. Kéuih tóuh m̀h-tóuh-ngoh a?   (tóuh-ngoh 肚餓)
   佢 肚 唔 肚 餓 呀 ？

4. Yìh-gā géi-dím a?   (yāt-dím-sàam 1:15)
   而 家 幾 點 呀 ？

5. Kéuih béi dihn-wá bīn-go a?   (tùhng-sih 同事)
   佢 畀 電 話 邊 個 呀 ？

6. Kéuih tīng-yaht fàan m̀h-fàan-gùng a?   (m̀h-fàan-gùng 唔返工)
   佢 聽 日 返 唔 返 工 呀 ？

III.

1. chāt-dím-yih 7:10   4. m̀h-haih 唔係
2. sahp-yāt-dím-sàam 11:15   5. haih 係
3. tùhng-sih 同事   6. m̀h-haih 唔係

LESSON 10

Review Exercise

I. *Fill in the blanks*

1. yám 飲   4. māt-yéh 乜嘢
2. m̀h-séung 唔想   5. jùng m̀h-jùng-yi sihk 鍾唔鍾意食
3. m̀h-yám 唔飲   6. dihn-wá 電話 (or any object)

II. *Rewrite sentences*

1. Kéuih pàhng-yáuh séung máaih sāam.
   佢 朋 友 想 買 衫 。

2. Néih yám m̀h-yám ga-fē a?
   你 飲 唔 飲 咖 啡 呀 ？

3. Chàhn sìn-sàang m̀h-jùng-yi tái hei.
   陳 先 生 唔 鍾 意 睇 戲 。

4. Néih séung tùhng bīn-go sihk faahn a?
   你 想 同 邊 個 食 飯 呀 ？

5. Néih sīng-kèih-yaht jùng-yi jouh māt-yéh a?
   你 星 期 日 想 做 乜 嘢 呀 ？

III. *Translation*

1. Néih séung yiu māt-yéh a?
   你 想 要 乜 嘢 呀 ？

2. M̀h-gòi béi sei-wún faahn ngóh.
   唔 該 畀 四 碗 飯 我 。

3. Ngóh m̀h-jùng-yi tùhng Chàhn sàang tái hei.
   我 唔 鍾 意 同 陳 生 睇 戲 。

4. Ngóh séung yiu yāt-būi séui.
   我 想 要 一 杯 水 。

5. Kéuih séung màaih dihn-sin.
   佢 想 買 電 視 。

6. Néih tīng-yaht heui m̀h-heui yám-chàh a?
   你 聽 日 去 唔 去 飲 茶 呀 ？

7. Néih sīng-kèih-yaht séung heui bīn-douh a?
   你 星 期 日 想 去 邊 度 呀 ？

8. Néih jùng-yi sihk māt-yéh a?
   你 鍾 意 食 乜 嘢 呀 ？

Listening Exercise

I. *(Track 119)*

1. Kéuih jùng-yi yám māt-yéh a? (yiht ga-fē 熱咖啡)
   佢 鍾 意 飲 乜 嘢 呀 ？

2. Kéuih-deih géi-dō go yàhn a? (sàam go 三個)
   佢 哋 幾 多 個 人 呀 ？

3. Kéuih-deih yám māt-yéh chàh a? (bóu-léi 普洱)
   佢 哋 飲 乜 嘢 茶 呀 ？

4. Kéuih-deih sihk m̀h-sihk náaih-wòhng-bāau a? (m̀h-sihk 唔食)
   佢 哋 食 唔 食 奶 皇 包 呀 ？

5. Kéuih séung m̀h-séung sihk chà-sìu-bāau a? (séung 想)
   佢 想 唔 想 食 叉 燒 包 呀 ？

II. *(Track 120)*

1. Néih-deih tīng-yaht heui yám chàh àh? (m̀h-haih 唔係)
   你 哋 聽 日 去 飲 茶 吖 ？

2. Yáuh géi-dō go pàhng-yáuh heui a? (sei go 四個)
   有 幾 多 個 朋 友 去 呀 ？

3. Néih-deih géi-dím heui yám chàh a? (yāt-dím-bun 1:30)
   你 哋 幾 點 去 飲 茶 呀 ？

4. Yáuh móuh sihk sài-máih-louh a? (móuh 冇)
   有 冇 食 西 米 露 呀 ？

5. Dī dím-sām hóu m̀h-hóu a? (hóu 好)
   啲 點 心 好 唔 好 呀 ？

6. Néih-deih géi-dím fàan ūk-kéi a? (sàam-dím 3:00)
   你 哋 幾 點 返 屋 企 呀 ？

LESSON 11

Review Exercise

Translation

1. Ngóh móuh béi bún syù kéuih.
   我 冇 畀 本 書 佢 。

2. Ngóh móuh heui gó-douh.
   我 冇 去 嗰 度 。

3. Ngóh pàhng-yáuh kàhm-máahn sahp-yāt-dím-sàam fan-gaau.
   我 朋 友 琴 晚 十 一 點 三 瞓 覺 。

4. Ngóh-deih yíng-jó hóu dò séung.
   我 哋 影 咗 好 多 相 。

5. Kéuih taai-táai m̀h-sái máaih-yéh.
   佢 太 太 唔 使 買 嘢 。

6. Ngóh yám-jó léuhng būi chàh.
   我 飲 咗 兩 杯 茶 。

7. Néih bé-jó jèung dāan bīn-go a?
   你 畀 咗 張 單 邊 個 呀 ？

8. Ngóh-deih sihk-jó hóu dò dím-sām. Dī dím-sām hóu hóu-sihk.
   我 哋 食 咗 好 多 點 心 。 啲 點 心 好 好 食 。

9. Ngóh tīng-yaht yiu fàan ūk-kéi sihk faahn.
   我 聽 日 要 返 屋 企 食 飯 。

10. Ngóh-deih móuh daap deih-tit heui Jùng-wàahn.
    我 哋 冇 搭 地 鐵 去 中 環 。

Listening Exersise

1. Néih-deih yáuh géi-dō wái a?   (a)
   你 哋 有 幾 多 位 呀 ？

2. Bīn-go dehng-tói a?   (c)
   邊 個 訂 枱 呀 ？

3. Néih séung yiu māt-yéh a?   (c)
   你 想 要 乜 嘢 呀 ？

4. Néih yiu géi-dō jek a?   (d)
   你 要 幾 多 隻 呀 ？

5. Néih séung sihk māt-yéh a?   (b)
   你 想 食 乜 嘢 呀 ？

6. Néih yiu géi-dō hā a?   (d)
   你 要 幾 多 蝦 呀 ？

7. Néih séung sihk māt-yéh hā a?   (a)
   你 想 食 乜 嘢 蝦 呀 ？

8. Yāt gàn hā géi-dō chín a?   (c)
   一 斤 蝦 幾 多 錢 呀 ？

LESSON 12

Review Exercise

I. Rewrite Sentences

1. Ngóh ge gūng-sī hái sahp-baat láu.
   我 嘅 公 司 喺 十 八 樓 。

2. Néih hái bīn-douh jyuh a?
   你 喺 邊 度 住 呀 ？

3. Nī-gàan gūng-sī m̀h-hái Jùng-wàahn.
   呢 間 公 司 唔 喺 中 環 。

4. Bīn-go hái Wāan-jái fàan-gùng a?
   邊 個 喺 灣 仔 返 工 呀 ？

5. Ngóh ge pàhng-yáuh hái Jìm-sà-jéui jyuh.
   我 嘅 朋 友 喺 尖 沙 咀 住 。

6. Léih sìn-sàang hái sàam láu yám chàh.
李 先 生 喺 三 樓 飲 茶 。

7. Ngóh m̀h-hái Tùhng-lòh-wāan jyuh.
我 唔 喺 銅 鑼 灣 住 。

II. *Translation*

1. Néih jùng m̀h-jùng-yi nī-gàan jáu-làuh a?
你 鍾 唔 鍾 意 呢 間 酒 樓 呀 ？

2. Ngóh hái Jìm-sà-jéui jyuh.
我 喺 尖 沙 咀 住 。

3. Néih pàhng-yáuh hái bīn-douh fàan-gùng a?
你 朋 友 喺 邊 度 返 工 呀 ？

4. Ngóh gàm-yaht hái ūk-kéi sihk faahn.
我 今 日 喺 屋 企 食 飯 。

5. Néih léuhng-dím-bun hái bīn-douh a?
你 兩 點 半 喺 邊 度 呀 ？

6. Ngóh gūng-sī hái yah-ńgh láu.
我 公 司 喺 廿 五 樓 。

7. Ngóh tùhng pàhng-yáuh hái Wāan-jái sihk faahn.
我 同 朋 友 喺 灣 仔 食 飯 。

8. Chàhn sìn-sàang kàhm-yaht hái bīn-douh a?
陳 先 生 琴 日 喺 邊 度 呀 ？

9. Ngóh móuh hái Tùhng-lòh-wāan máaih-yéh.
我 冇 喺 銅 鑼 灣 買 嘢 。

10. Jáu-làuh hái bīn-douh a?
酒 樓 喺 邊 度 呀 ？

11. Néih-deih géi-dím hái mùhn-háu dáng a?
我 哋 幾 點 喺 門 口 等 呀 ？

12. Gàm-máahn jàn-haih yiht.
今 晚 真 係 熱 。

III.

1. m̀h-haih, haih B1
   唔係，係 B 1

2. yih láu 二樓

3. haih 係

4. ngāam 啱

5. B1

6. móuh tùhng-jōng 冇童裝

7. yáuh 有

8. ngāam 啱

9. luhk láu 六樓

10. ńgh láu 五樓

V.

A.

1. Géi-dō chín a? 幾多錢呀？

2. Géi-dō dím a? 幾多點呀？

3. Géi-dō houh bā-sí a? 幾多號巴士呀？

4. Géi-(dō) yuht a? 幾（多）月呀？

5. Gàm-yaht géi-dō houh a? 今日幾多號呀？

6. Géi-dō jit a? 幾多折呀？

7. Gó-douh yáuh géi-dō yàhn a? 嗰度有幾多人呀？

8. Géi-dō wún faahn a? 幾多碗飯呀？

9. Géi-dō go pàhng-yáuh làih a? 幾多個朋友嚟呀？

10. Géi-dō būi ga-fē a? 幾多杯咖啡呀？

11. Géi-dō gwun bē-jáu a? 幾多罐啤酒呀？

12. Géi-dō bún syù a? 幾多本書呀？

13. Néih géi-sìh/ géi yuht géi houh sāang-yaht a?
    你幾時/幾月幾號生日呀？

14. Sīng-kèih-géi heui yám chàh a? 星期幾去飲茶呀？

15. Néih dihn-wá géi-dō houh a? 你電話幾多號呀？

B.

1. Māt-yéh sīk a? 乜嘢色呀？
2. Néih daap māt-yéh chē a? 你搭乜嘢車呀？
3. Néih yiu māt-yéh a? 你要乜嘢呀？
4. Néih sīng-kèih-luhk jouh māt-yéh a? 你星期六做乜嘢呀？
5. Néih jùng-yi sihk māt-yéh a? 你鍾意食乜嘢呀？
6. Yám māt-yéh chèh a? 飲乜嘢茶呀？

C.

1. Hái bīn-douh a? 喺邊度呀？
2. Bīn-būi haih chàh, bīn-būi haih ga-fē a? 邊杯係茶，邊杯係咖啡呀？
3. Bīn-dī sāam haih néih ga? 邊啲衫係你㗎？
4. Bīn-go a? / Bīn-wái a? 邊個呀？／邊位呀？
5. Bīn-go tùhng-sih a? 邊個同事呀？
6. Néih bīn yaht dāk-hàahn a? 你邊日得閒呀？

D.

1. Hái douh sihk dihng līng-jáu a? 喺度食定拎走呀？
2. Yiht dihng dung a? 熱定凍呀？
3. Daaih-dī dihng sai-dī a? 大啲定細啲呀？
4. Hùhng-sīk dihng làahm-sīk a? 紅色定藍色呀？
5. Gàm-yaht dihng tīng-yaht a? 今日定聽日呀？
6. Néih dihng ngóh a? 你定我呀？
7. Méih-gwok dihng Jùng-gwok a? 美國定中國呀？
8. Jùng-wàahn dihng Tùhng-lòh-wāan a? 中環定銅鑼灣呀？

Listening Exercise

I *(Track 145)*

1. Chàhn sìn-sàang heui bīn-douh a?　　　(Gām-jūng 金鐘)
   陳　先　生　去　邊　度　呀　？

2. Kéuih heui Gām-jūng jouh māt-yéh a?   (máaih-yéh 買嘢)
    佢 去 金 鐘 做 乜 嘢 呀 ？

3. Chàhn sìn-sàang haih néih bīn-go a?   (pàhng-yáuh 朋友)
    陳 先 生 係 你 邊 個 呀 ？

4. Néih hóu ma?   (hóu 好)
    你 好 嗎 ？

5. Néih hái bīn-douh jyuh a?   (Tùhng-lòh-wāan 銅鑼灣)
    你 喺 邊 度 住 呀 ？

6. Chàhn síu-jé séung tùhng néih jouh māt-yéh a?   (yám chàh 飲茶)
    陳 小 姐 想 同 你 做 乜 嘢 呀 ？

7. Néih dāk m̀h-dāk-hàahn heui a?   (m̀h-dāk-hàahn 唔得閒)
    你 得 唔 得 閒 去 呀 ？

8. Néih yiu jouh māt-yéh a?   (fàan-gùng 返工)
    你 要 做 乜 嘢 呀 ？

II.

1. a   2. b   3. d

LESSON 13

B. Practice

1. Ngóh sìh-sìh heui Jùng-wàahn tái hei.
    我 時 時 去 中 環 睇 戲 。

2. Ngóh hóu-síu heui Wohng-gok máaih-yéh.
    我 好 少 去 旺 角 買 嘢 。

3. Ngóh yáuh-sìh tái dihn-sih.
    我 有 時 睇 電 視 。

4. Ngóh sìh-sìh hòi-wúi.
    我 時 時 開 會 。

5. Ngóh yáuh-sìh heui léuih-hàhng.
我 有 時 去 旅 行 。

6. Ngóh sìh-sìh daap dīk-sí fàan-gùng.
我 時 時 搭 的 士 返 工 。

7. Ngóh hóu-síu m̀h-séuhng-tòhng.
我 好 少 唔 上 堂 。

8. Baat-yuht sìh-sìh lohk-yúh.
八 月 時 時 落 雨 。

Review Exercise

I.   Rewrite sentences

1. Ngóh luhk-yuht heui-jó léuih-hàhng.
我 六 月 去 咗 旅 行 。

2. Nī-go láih-baai-sàam sei-dím hòi-wúi.
呢 個 禮 拜 三 四 點 開 會 。

3. Kàhm-yaht hóu m̀h-hóu-tìn a?
琴 日 好 唔 好 天 呀 ？

4. Ngóh sīng-kèih yih m̀h-dāk-hàahn, daahn-haih sīng-kèih-sei dāk-hàahn.
我 星 期 二 唔 得 閒 ， 但 係 星 期 四 得 閒 。

5. Ngóh-deih tīng-yaht heui léuih-hàhng hóu m̀h-hóu a?
我 哋 聽 日 去 旅 行 好 唔 好 呀 ？

6. Gàm-yaht ge tìn-hei hóu syù-fuhk.
今 日 嘅 天 氣 好 舒 服 。

II.   Translation

1. Ngóh-deih baat-yuht hóu-síu heui léuih-hàhng
我 哋 八 月 好 少 去 旅 行 。

2. Seuhng-go láih-baai móuh lohk-yúh.
上 個 禮 拜 冇 落 雨 。

3. Hah-go sīng-kèih-yāt hòi-wúi, daahn-haih ngóh m̀h-dāk-hàahn heui.
   下 個 星 期 一 開 會 ， 但 係 我 唔 得 閒 去 。

4. Néih hah-go sīng-kèih-luhk heui bīn-douh a?
   你 下 個 星 期 六 去 邊 度 呀 ？

5. Yih-yuht jeui dung.
   二 月 最 凍 。

6. Ngóh yáuh-sìh tùhng tùhng-sih sihk faahn, yáuh-sìh tùhng pàhng-yàuh sihk.
   我 有 時 同 同 事 食 飯 ， 有 時 同 朋 友 食 。

7. Sīng-kéih-ńgh hóu hóu-tìn, daahn-haih sīng-kèih-luhk lohk yúh.
   星 期 五 好 好 天 ， 但 係 星 期 六 落 雨 。

8. Ngóh sìh-sìh hái gūng-sī sihk faahn.
   我 時 時 喺 公 司 食 飯 。

9. Sei-yuht yah-sàam houh fong m̀h-fong-ga a?
   四 月 廿 三 號 放 唔 放 假 呀 ？

10. Ngóh sīng-kèih-yāt dou sīng-kèih-ńgh fàan-gùng. Sīng-kèih-luhk heui
    máaih-yéh. Sīng-kèih-yaht hái ūk-kéi fan-gaau.
    我 星 期 一 至 星 期 五 返 工 。 星 期 六 去 買
    嘢 。 星 期 日 喺 屋 企 瞓 覺 。

11. Seuhng-go sīng-kèih-yih yàm-tìn.
    上 個 星 期 二 陰 天 。

12. Sahp-yāt-yuht ge tìn-hei hóu syù-fuhk.
    十 一 月 嘅 天 氣 好 舒 服 。

IV.

1. 18°C
2. 20°C
3. 32°C
4. 22°C
5. 25°C
6. m̀h-haih 唔係
7. haih 係
8. m̀h-haih 唔係
9. 17°C
10. m̀h-dung 唔凍

V.

1. hóu-tìn 好天

2. móuh 冇

3. m̀h-haih 唔係，lohk-yúh 落雨

4. haih 係

5. m̀h-haih 唔係，lohk-yúh 落雨

6. m̀h-haih 唔係，hóu-tìn 好天

7. yih-sahp-houh hóu-tìn 二十號好天，
   daahn-haih yih-sahp-sei-houh yàm-tìn 但係二十四號陰天

8. móuh 冇

9. hóu-tìn 好天

10. m̀h-haih 唔係，tìng-yaht lohk-yúh 聽日落雨

Listening Exercise   *(Track 160)*

1. Gām-yaht láih-baai-géi a?   (láih-baai-sàam 禮拜三)
   今 日 禮 拜 幾 呀 ？

2. Gām-yaht géi-dō douh a?   (30℃)
   今 日 幾 多 度 呀 ？

3. Sīng-kèih-géi jeui yiht a?   (sīng-kèih-yāt 星期一)
   星 期 幾 最 熱 呀 ？

4. Hah go sīng-kèih-sei fong-ga, haih m̀h-haih a?   (haih 係)
   下 個 星 期 四 放 假 ， 係 唔 係 呀 ？

5. Néih fong-ga haih m̀h-haih hái ūk-kéi a?   (haih 係)
   你 放 假 係 唔 係 喺 屋 企 呀 ？

6. Néih hái ūk-kéi jouh māt-yéh a?   (fan-gaau 瞓覺)
   你 喺 屋 企 做 乜 嘢 呀 ？

7. Néih jeui jùng-yi jouh māt-yéh a?   (fan-gaau 瞓覺)
   你 最 鍾 意 做 乜 嘢 呀 ？

8. Nī go láih-baai ge tìn-hei hóu m̀h-hóu a?　　　(m̀h-hóu 唔好)
　　呢　個　禮　拜　嘅　天　氣　好　唔　好　呀　?

9. Yìh-gā yáuh móuh lohk-yúh a?　　　　　　　(móuh 冇)
　　而　家　有　冇　落　雨　呀　?

10. Gām-yaht ge tìn-hei dím a?　　　　　(màh-má-déi 麻麻哋)
　　今　日　嘅　天　氣　點　呀　?

LESSON 14

Practice

A.

1. Dihn-wá hái bín-douh?
　電　話　邊　度　?

2. Sìn-sàang hái bín-douh?
　先　生　喺　邊　度　?

3. Néih pàhng-yáuh hái bīn-gàan jáu-dim jyuh a?
　你　朋　友　喺　邊　間　酒　店　住　呀　?

4. Néih hái bīn-gàan chāan-tēng sihk faahn a?
　你　喺　邊　間　餐　廳　食　飯　呀　?

5. Jeui káhn ge deih-tit jaahm hái bīn-douh a?
　最　近　嘅　地　鐵　站　喺　邊　度　呀　?

B.

1. Ngóh jì sahp-ńgh láu yáuh yāt gāan chāan-tēng.
　我　知　十　五　樓　有　一　間　餐　廳　。

2. Kéuih sīk ngóh pàhng-yáuh.
　佢　識　我　朋　友　。

3. Ngóh m̀h-jì Hàhng-sāng Ngàhn-hòhng hái bīn-douh.
　我　唔　知　恒　生　銀　行　喺　邊　度　。

4. Ngóh m̀h-sīk heui gó-douh.
   我 唔 識 去 嗰 度 。

5. Ngóh m̀h-sīk tái Jùng-màhn.
   我 唔 識 睇 中 文 。

Review Exercise

I. *Fill in the blanks*

1. sīk, sīk 識，識

2. Yùh-gwó, jauh
   如果，就

3. deih-tit 地鐵

4. Yùh-gwó, jauh 如果，就

5. jauh fan-gaau 就瞓覺

6. Yùh-gwó m̀h-sihk faahn
   如果唔食飯

II. *Translation*

1. Ngóh tùhng-sih hái fuk-gahn jyuh.
   我 同 事 喺 附 近 住 。

2. Ngóh m̀h-sīk Wòhng sìn-sàang.
   我 唔 識 黃 先 生 。

3. Yùh-gwó néih séung máaih Yīng-màhn syù, heui gó-gāan pou-táu máaih lā.
   如 果 你 想 買 英 文 書 ， 去 嗰 間 舖 頭 買 啦 。

4. Ngóh jì kéuih haih Léih taai-táai ge pàhng-yáuh.
   我 知 佢 係 李 太 太 嘅 朋 友 。

5. Jó-mihn ge mùhn-háu heui gàai-síh.
   左 面 嘅 門 口 去 街 市 。

6. Ngóh hái gó-gàan ngàhn-hòhng chìhn-mihn daap dīk-sí.
   我 喺 嗰 間 銀 行 前 面 搭 的 士 。

7. Jùng-wàahn yáuh hóu-dò hóu ge chāan-tēng.
   中 環 有 好 多 好 嘅 餐 廳 。

8. Deui-mihn yáuh léuhng gàan jáu-dim.
   對 面 有 兩 間 酒 店 。

9. Kéuih gūng-sī hái gó-dī pou-táu hauh-mihn.
   佢 公 司 喺 嗰 啲 舖 頭 後 面 。

10. Nī-douh móuh síu-bā.
    呢 度 冇 小 巴 。

IV.

1. jó-mihn 左面

2. sé-jih-làuh ge deui-mihn 寫字樓嘅對面

3. ngàhn-hòhng ge yauh-mihn 銀行嘅右面

4. pou-táu ge yauh-mihn 舖頭嘅右面

5. yáuh 有

6. ngàhn-hòhng ge hauh-mihn 銀行嘅後面

7. jáu-táu 酒樓

8. gàai síh 街市

9. deui-mihn 對面

10. pou-táu ge hauh-mihn 舖頭嘅後面

11. móuh 冇

12. yauh-mihn 右面

Listening Exercise *(Track 172)*

1. Néih sīk m̀h-sīk Chàhn táai a?   (sīk 識)
   你 識 唔 識 陳 太 呀 ？

2. Chàhn táai haih néih bīn-go a?   (tùhng-sih 同事)
   陳 太 係 你 邊 個 呀 ？

3. Gáu-lùhng Jáu-dim hái m̀h-hái Jìm-sà-jéui a?   (haih 係)
   九 龍 酒 店 喺 唔 喺 尖 沙 咀 呀 ？

4. Nī-gàan jáu-dim hái Hèung-góng Jáu-dim ge   (m̀h-haih 唔係)
   gaak-lèih (*by the side) àh?
   呢 間 酒 店 喺 香 港 酒 店 嘅 隔 籬 吖 ？

5. Nī-gàan jáu-dim hái Gáu-lùhng Jáu-dim ge   (yauh-mihn 右面)
   bīn-mihn a?
   呢 間 酒 店 喺 九 龍 酒 店 嘅 邊 面 呀 ？

6. Gām-jūng yáuh móuh Seibu a?   (yáuh 有)
   金 鐘 有 冇 Seibu 呀 ？

7. Seibu hái Gām-jūng ge bīn-douh a?   (Taai-gwú Gwóng-chèuhng)
   Seibu 喺 金 鐘 嘅 邊 度 呀 ？   （太古廣場）

8. Taai-gwú Gwóng-chèuhng (*Pacific Place) hái   (deui-mihn 對面)
   Gām-jūng-lòhng (*Queensway Plaza) ge bīn-mihn a?
   太 古 廣 場 喺 金 鐘 廊 嘅 邊 面 呀 ？

9. Tīng-yaht hái chāan-tēng sihk faahn àh?   (m̀h-haih 唔係)
   聽 日 喺 餐 廳 食 飯 吖 ？

10. Hái bīn-douh ge jáu-làuh sihk faahn a ?   (Hèung-góng Jáu-dim
    喺 邊 度 嘅 酒 樓 食 飯 呀 ？   （香港酒店）

11. Néih-deih géi-dím dáng a?   (baat-dím 8:00)
    你 哋 幾 點 等 呀 ？

12. Hái bīn-douh dáng a?   (Tùhng-lòh-wāan deih-tit-jaahm
    喺 邊 度 等 呀 ？   Hàhng-sāng Ngàhn-hòhng)
        （銅鑼灣地鐵站恆生銀行）

LESSON 15

C. Practice

1. Néih wúih m̀h-wúih hái Gām-jūng sihk faahn a?
   你 會 唔 會 喺 金 鐘 食 飯 吖 ？

2. Hah-go sīng-kèih wúih m̀h-wúih hóu-tìn a?
   下 個 星 期 會 唔 會 好 天 呀 ？

3. Néih hah-go sīng-kèih-luhk wúih m̀h-wúih tùhng pàhng-yáuh heui máaih-
   你 下 個 星 期 六 會 唔 會 同 朋 友 去 買
   yéh a?
   嘢 呀 ？

4. Néih tīng-yaht géi-dím wúih hái ūk-kéi a?
   你 聽 日 幾 點 會 喺 屋 企 呀 ？

5. Néih wúih tùhng bīnò-go heui léuih-hàhng a?
   你 會 同 邊 個 去 旅 行 呀 ？

6. Ngóh-deih géi-sìh wúih hòi-wúi a?
   我 哋 幾 時 會 開 會 呀 ？

Review Exercise

I. Translation

1. Ngóh pàhng-yáuh wúih hohk Gwóng-dùng-wá.
   我 朋 友 會 學 廣 東 話 。

2. Néih jouh-gán māt-yéh a?
   你 做 緊 乜 嘢 呀 ？

3. Ngóh hóu mòhng, yāt-jahn kìng lā.
   我 好 忙 ， 一 陣 傾 啦 。

4. Néih dáng-jó ngóh géi-noih la?
   你 等 咗 我 幾 耐 喇 ？

5. Ngóh hái nī-douh sàam-nìhn la.
   我 喺 呢 度 三 年 喇 。

6. Néih tùhng bīn-go kìng-gán a?
   你 同 邊 個 傾 緊 呀 ？

7. Néih sihk faahn sihk géi-noih ga?
   你 食 飯 食 幾 耐 㗎 ？

8. Néih máaih-jó nī-go dihn-sih géi-noih a?
   你 買 咗 呢 個 電 視 幾 耐 呀 ？

9. Néih pìhng-sìh dāk-hàahn jouh māt-yéh a?
   你 平 時 得 閒 做 乜 嘢 呀 ？

10. Ngóh nám-jó yāt fàn-jùng.
    我 諗 咗 一 分 鐘 。

11. Sīng-kèih-ńgh wúih m̀h-wúih lohk-yúh a?
    星　期　五　會　唔　會　落　雨　呀　？

12. Ngóh sīng-kèih-yaht wúih heui Jìm-sà-jéui máaih yéh. Néih làih m̀h-làih a?
    我　星　期　日　會　去　尖　沙　咀　買　嘢　。　你　嚟　唔　嚟　呀　？

III.　*Review on 'yih'* 二 *and 'léuhng'* 兩

1. léuhng go sīng-kèih 兩個星期

2. léuhng-dím-yih 兩點二

3. yāt-yuht yih houh 一月二號

4. léuhng go jùng-tàuh yih-sahp fàn-jùng 兩個鐘頭二十分鐘

5. léuhng-go-yih 兩個二

6. hah-go sīng-kèih-yih 下個星期二

7. yih-baak-yih-sahp bún syù 二百二十本書

8. yih-maahn yih-chìn yih-baak yih-sahp-yih mān
   二萬二千二百二十二蚊

9. yih-sahp-yih go yàhn 二十二個人

10. léuhng būi chàh 兩杯茶

11. léuhng mān 兩蚊

12. yih-chìn bún syù 二千本書

13. yih-lìhng-yāt-yih nìhn yih-yuht yih houh 二零一二年二月二號

14. yih-baak-lìhng-yih fàn-jùng 二百零二分鐘

15. yih-baak yāt-sahp-yih go yuht 二百一十二個月

16. yih-baak nìhn 二百年

IV.

1. nī-go sīng-kèih-sàam heui Jìm-sā-jéui, hah-go sīng-kèih-sei heui Wāan-
   呢 個 星 期 三 去 尖 沙 咀 ， 下 個 星 期 四 去 灣
   jái.
   仔 。

2. pàhng-yáuh 朋友

3. tái hei 睇戲

4. Gām-jūng 金鐘

5. heui 去

6. tùhng-sih 同事

7. yāt go jùng-tàuh 一個鐘頭

8. gūng-sī 公司

9. Léih sìn-sàang, sahp-yih-dim-bun 李先生，十二點半

10. tái syù 睇書

LESSON 16

A. Practice

Translate and answer the questions

1. Néih yáuh móuh tái-gwo nī-tou hei a?
   你 有 冇 睇 過 呢 套 戲 呀 ？

2. Néih yáuh móuh hohk-gwo Jùng-màhn a?
   你 有 冇 學 過 中 文 呀 ？

3. Néih yáuh móuh heui-gwo gó-gàan cháan-tēng a?
   你 有 冇 去 過 嗰 間 餐 廳 呀 ？

4. Néih yáuh móuh tùhng kéuih kìng-gwo a?
   你 有 冇 同 佢 傾 過 呀 ？

5. Néih kàhm-máahn yáuh móuh fan-gwo gaau a? Fan-jó géi-dò go jùng-
   你 琴 晚 有 冇 瞓 過 覺 呀 ？ 瞓 咗 幾 多 個 鐘
   tàuh a?
   頭 呀 ？

6. Néih yáuh móuh jyuh-gwo Jìm-sā-jéui ge Hèung-góng Jáu-dim a?
你 有 冇 住 過 尖 沙 咀 嘅 香 港 酒 店 呀 ？

B. Practice

Translate and answer the questions

1. Néih tóuh-ngoh meih a?
你 肚 餓 未 呀 ？

2. Néih sihk-jó faahn meih a?
你 食 咗 飯 未 呀 ？

3. Néih máaih-jó gó-bún syù meih a ?
你 買 咗 嗰 本 書 未 呀 ？

4. Néih béi-jó dihn-wá tùhng-sih meih a?
你 畀 咗 電 話 同 事 未 呀 ？

5. Néih heui-jó ngàhn-hòhng meih a?
你 去 咗 銀 行 未 呀 ？

6. Néih dāk-hàahn meih a? Ngóh yiu dáng géi-noih a?
你 得 閒 未 呀 ？ 我 要 等 幾 耐 呀 ？

C. Practice

Translate and answer the questions

1. Gó-douh jyun m̀h-jyun dāk jó a?
嗰 度 轉 唔 轉 得 左 呀 ？

2. Néih sihk m̀h-sihk-dāk laaht a?
你 食 唔 食 得 辣 呀 ？

3. Ngóh sahp-yih-dím jì-hauh béi dihn-wá néih dāk m̀h dāk a? Néih fan-
我 十 二 點 之 後 畀 電 話 你 得 唔 得 呀 ？ 你 瞓

gaau meih a?
覺 未 呀 ？

4. Néih yám m̀h-yám-dāk bē-jáu a ?

你 飲 唔 飲 得 啤 酒 呀 ?

Review Exercise

I.   Translation

1. Néih heui-gwo gó-gàan jáu-làuh yám-chàh meih a?

你 去 過 嗰 間 酒 樓 飲 茶 未 呀 ?

2. Ngóh gei-dāk, daahn-haih ngóh meih jouh.

我 記 得 ， 但 係 我 未 做 。

3. Néih daap-gwo deih-tit meih a?

你 搭 過 地 鐵 未 呀 ?

4. Ngóh meih heui-gwo néih ūk-kéi.

我 未 去 過 你 屋 企 。

5. Kéuih m̀h-syù-fuhk. Kéuih gàm-yaht m̀h-hòi-dāk-wúi.

佢 唔 舒 服 。 佢 今 日 唔 開 得 會 。

6. Nī-yeuhng yéh tìhm dihng hàahm ga?

呢 樣 嘢 甜 定 鹹 㗎 ?

7. Néih sihk sìn lā. Ngóh m̀h-tóuh-ngoh.

你 食 先 啦 。 我 唔 肚 餓 。

8. Ngóh yiu tèng dihn-wá sìn. Ngóh-deih yāt-jahn kìng.

我 要 聽 電 話 先 。 我 哋 一 陣 傾 。

9. Nī-douh m̀h-jihk-heui-dāk. Néih yiu jyun jó.

呢 度 唔 直 去 得 。 你 要 轉 左 。

10. Ngóh meih gin-gwo kéuih. Kéuih haih bīn-go a?

我 未 見 過 佢 。 佢 係 邊 個 呀 ?

11. Kéuih meih fàan ūk-kéi.

佢 未 返 屋 企 。

12. Néih yáuh móuh tái-gwo gó-tou hei a? Ngóh tái-gwo léuhng chi.

你 有 冇 睇 過 嗰 套 戲 ? 我 睇 過 兩 次 。

IV.

Translate the questions

1. Néih géi-dím héi-sān ga?
   你 幾 點 起 身 㗎 ？

2. Néih jìu-jóu sihk m̀h sihk yéh ga?
   你 朝 早 食 唔 食 嘢 㗎 ？

3. Néih géi-dím fàan-gùng a?
   你 幾 點 返 工 呀 ？

4. Néih dím-yéung fàan-gùng ga? Haih m̀h haih daap dīk-sí a?
   你 點 樣 返 工 㗎 ？ 係 唔 係 搭 的 士 呀 ？

5. Néih gūng-sī hái bīn-douh a?
   你 公 司 喺 邊 度 呀 ？

6. Néih sīng-kèih-luhk sái m̀h-sái fàan-gùng ga?
   你 星 期 六 使 唔 使 返 工 㗎 ？

7. Néih géi-dím sihk aan a?
   你 幾 點 食 晏 呀 ？

8. Néih pìhng-sìh hái bīn-douh sihk faahn a?
   你 平 時 喺 邊 度 食 飯 呀 ？

9. Jùng m̀h jùng-yi yám chàh a?
   鍾 唔 鍾 意 飲 茶 呀 ？

10. Géi-dím sàu-gùng a?
    幾 點 收 工 呀 ？

11. Néih jáu ge sìh-hauh tùhng tùhng-sih góng māt-yéh a?
    你 走 嘅 時 候 同 同 事 講 乜 嘢 呀 ？

12. Néih kàhm-yaht sàu-gùng jì-hauh jouh māt-yéh a?
    你 琴 日 收 工 之 後 做 乜 嘢 呀 ？

13. Néih jùng m̀h jùng-yi tùhng pàhng-yáuh yám-yéh a?
    你 鍾 唔 鍾 意 同 朋 友 飲 嘢 呀 ？

14. Néih géi dím fàan ūk-kéi a?
    你 幾 點 返 屋 企 呀 ？

15. Néih daap māt-yéh chē fàan ūk-kéi a?
    你 搭 乜 嘢 車 返 屋 企 呀 ？

16. Néih hái bīn-douh jyuh a? Jyuh géi-dō láu a ?
    你 喺 邊 度 住 呀 ？ 住 幾 多 樓 呀 ？

17. Néih géi-dím sihk máahn-faahn a?
    你 幾 點 食 晚 飯 呀 ？

18. Néih tùhng bīn-go sihk faahn a?
    你 同 邊 個 食 飯 呀 ？

19. Néih sihk faahn ge sìh-hauh tái m̀h-tái dihn-sih a?
    你 食 飯 嘅 時 候 睇 唔 睇 電 視 呀 ？

20. Néih géi-sìh chēut heui sihk faahn a?
    你 幾 時 出 去 食 飯 呀 ？

21. Néih gàm-máahn séung m̀h séung sihk chà-sìu faahn a?
    你 今 晚 想 唔 想 食 叉 燒 飯 呀 ？

22. Néih géi-dím fan-gaau a?
    你 幾 點 瞓 覺 呀 ？

23. Néih dāk-hàahn jùng-yi jouh māt-yéh a?
    你 得 閒 鍾 意 做 乜 嘢 呀 ？

24. Néih jùng m̀h-jùng-yi máaih-yéh a? Néih sìh-sìh heui Tùhng-lòh-wāan
    māaih-yéh àh?
    你 鍾 唔 鍾 意 買 嘢 呀 ？ 你 時 時 去 銅 鑼 灣 買
    嘢 吖 ？